Ask about Santa Fe

ASK ABOUT

464 Essential Questions and Their Answers about This City and the State of New Mexico

SANTA FE

James J. Raciti

SUNSTONE
PRESS

SANTA FE

Sunstone books may be purchased for educational, business, or sales promotional use.
For information please write: Special Markets Department, Sunstone Press,
P.O. Box 2321, Santa Fe, New Mexico 87504-2321.

Book and cover design › Vicki Ahl
Body typeface › Adobe Jenson Pro
Printed on acid-free paper
∞
eBook 978-1-61139-328-6

Library of Congress Cataloging-in-Publication Data

Raciti, James J., 1933-
   Ask about Santa Fe : 464 essential questions and their answers about this city and the
State of New Mexico / by James J. Raciti.
      pages cm
   Includes bibliographical references.
   ISBN 978-1-63293-030-9 (softcover : alk. paper)
   1. Santa Fe (N.M.)--History. 2. Santa Fe (N.M.)--Questions and answers. 3. New
Mexico--Questions and answers. I. Title. II. Title: 464 essential questions and their
answers about Santa Fe and the State of New Mexico. III. Title: 464 essential questions
and their answers about this city and the State of New Mexico.
   F804.S257R326 2015
   978.9'56--dc23
                          2014036239

WWW.SUNSTONEPRESS.COM
SUNSTONE PRESS / POST OFFICE BOX 2321 / SANTA FE, NM 87504-2321 /USA
(505) 988-4418 / ORDERS ONLY (800) 243-5644 / FAX (505) 988-1025

Contents

List of Illustrations

All illustrations from *All Trails Lead to Santa Fe,*
An Anthology Commemorating the 400th Anniversary of the Founding of
Santa Fe, New Mexico in 1610. Published by Sunstone Press in 2010.

On the Cover: View of the Exchange Hotel or La Fonda in Santa Fe, New Mexico. From *Harper's Weekly*, April 21, 1866.

Introduction

Here are four hundred sixty-four questions
and their answers about the State of New Mexico and
its capital Santa Fe from its origins to the present day,
information about the native peoples of the Southwest
and those Spanish explorers who made their mark on
the culture, language and religion of the regions of New
Mexico. More than four hundred years have passed since
the first settlers ventured into this new land, fought off the
marauding Indian tribes and endured the hardships of this
inhospitable country. The only successful Indian Revolt
in North America, the surprising turnabout giving the
forces of General Kearny a bloodless victory over Mexico
and the extraordinary development during the Battle of
Glorieta turning defeat into victory for the Union Forces
of the West all are topics in a history of enlightenment.
In *Ask About Santa Fe*, questions arise about the birth
of trade on the Santa Fe Trail, wars for dominance, the
history of religion, politics, population, resources, and the
remarkable people that lent their imagination, hard work
and dedication to the state.

1

The Beginnings

1. Where in the Santa Fe area were the first settlements of native people located?

The first settlements in the Santa Fe area were located in the Jemez Mountains. The valley was named "Valle Grande."

2. Where did these natives originate?

From our best information, they came from Chaco Canyon and Mesa Verde.

3. What made their settlement in the Jemez Mountains suitable for them?

About 1.2 million years ago, an ancient volcano erupted there, considered to be about 300 times stronger than Washington State's Mount St. Helens. The soft ash deposits were ideal for the creating of cave dwellings and interior tunnels.

4. What distinction does Santa Fe have in regards to its own age?

Santa Fe is the oldest capital in the United States. It is second only to St. Augustine, Florida as the oldest city in the country. This is true only in regards to cities established by European settlers.

5. What is the oldest pueblo in New Mexico?

The oldest pueblo in New Mexico is Acoma. It has been inhabited continuously since about 1075 A.D.

6. How large is the State of New Mexico?

Today, the State of New Mexico covers 121,666 square miles making it the fifth largest state in the Union.

7. Was the land mass of New Mexico larger at one time than it is at present?

When New Mexico was still a territory, it included all the land that now makes up the State of Arizona.

8. What are its present dimensions?

The state is an almost perfect rectangle; it measures 390 miles north to south and 350 miles east to west.

9. Where is Santa Fe located?

Santa Fe is located in the north-central quadrant of the state. It is considered to be in the high desert at an elevation of 7,000 feet, above sea level.

10. Is Santa Fe the highest point of the state?

No. To the north of Santa Fe, the elevation is higher. Taos, for example, is about 9,000 feet.

11. Why is New Mexico called the "Land of Poco Tiempo?"

Poco Tiempo means "little time." Some say that time means little here. Others say that New Mexico is the land of little time.

12. What does Santa Fe mean?

Santa Fe means "Holy Faith." The complete name is The Royal City of the Holy Faith of San Francisco d'Assisi.

13. Why is Santa Fe sometimes called the "City Different" instead of the "Different City?"

In the Spanish language adjectives mostly follow the nouns they modify.

14. What vegetation can be found in and around the capital city?

At the elevation of Santa Fe, snow falls in winter but melts quickly. There is an abundance of piñon and juniper trees. Above 8,000 feet, one finds the ponderosa pine, which gives way to the aspen at higher altitudes.

15. Is there abundant snowfall in Santa Fe?

Most of New Mexico is constantly in a state of drought. Santa Fe is no exception. There is snow but it is never enough, according to the skiers. New Mexico must rely on the rains during the summer months for most of its water. Precipitation is an important factor in the climate. In this, the entire state of New Mexico is deficient.

16. What wildlife can be found in the area of Santa Fe?

Wildlife around the Santa Fe area includes foxes, skunks, porcupines and sometimes larger animals like antelope, bighorn sheep and even bear. The ubiquitous coyote can be found in many of the neighborhoods of the city.

17. What are the major rivers in New Mexico?

The major rivers of New Mexico are the Rio Grande, Pecos, Canadian, San Juan and Gila. Water has always played an important role in the development of the state. The inhabitants prior to 1900 (when they learned to use ground water) had to rely only on water sources from the rivers.

18. What is the average annual precipitation for the state?

The annual average precipitation is only 15 inches, the mountains and the eastern part of the state having more rain and snow.

19. What is the annual average temperature in the state?

The mean annual temperature for the state is about 53 degrees Fahrenheit but can vary as much as 26 degrees at different locations.

20. What deficiencies did the Spanish settlers find in their new home?

The apparent deficiencies for the early settlers were the following: lack of rainfall, extreme isolation, lack of navigable rivers, lack of timber and lack of minerals in much of the region.

21. Of these deficiencies, what if anything has changed at the present time?

The lack of minerals has changed. Modern transportation has, however, made New Mexico less isolated than it was for the early settlers.

22. How well did the Spaniards understand the geography of this vast new land?

The early Spaniards had little knowledge of geography and assumed that the land of New Mexico was only a short day's overland journey from Florida. Distances were understood in terms of the distances they knew in Spain.

23. How did these settlers manage with the desert conditions of this country?

Lack of water plagued the early natives and settlers and continues to be a problem today. Centuries of Moorish occupation in Spain taught the Spaniards the importance of gathering water in cisterns below their houses. The early Spaniards in New Mexico carried this important information with them but over the centuries, it became lost or forgotten. Much of the rainfall we receive today runs off and is gone. Annually we remain badly prepared for the many months of drought. Because of sediment and silt, our storage capacities continue to decrease. We have become demanding and voracious in our need for water, unlike the early Americans who made judicious use of this precious resource.

2

The Early Americans

24. What are the earliest traces of human existence in New Mexico?

Evidence exists that humans lived in the Sandia area of New Mexico as early as 25,000 years before Christ. Basic tools and weapons of hunt were found near Clovis, New Mexico dating from 10,000 to 9,000 years before the Christian era.

25. Do we know the origin of the people who populated New Mexico?

We are not certain of the origins of the people who populated the land we now call New Mexico. Some believe they came from Asia over what is popularly called the "ice bridge" that joined Russia to Alaska, following the migrating herds. It is believed that these people migrated south over the plains searching for a more agreeable climate.

26. What other theories are there about these early origins?

Others believed they came from the south, land we now call Central America searching for richer soil for their crops. What we do know for certain is that these people, whatever their name or origin, lived on the land the Spaniards began to occupy as early as the 1500s.

27. By what name were these people known?

They were known by many names; principally they referred to themselves as "Our People," "Our Nation." The name that stands out historically is Anasazi. Curiously enough, this was not a name they gave to themselves but rather a term in the Navajo language, meaning enemy of our ancestors and later simply "ancient people."

28. How is the American Indian classified?

An arbitrary but useful classification of the American Indian may be made as follows: 1) by the language they speak; 2) by their physical or anatomical characteristics; 3) by the way they live. Because the Pueblo Indians preferred to build communities, till the land and remain in one place for long periods of time, they differed from the Plains Indians.

29. What special role did the Plains Indians play in the settlement of the Southwest?

The Plains Indians constituted for a much longer time than we realized the most effective barrier set up by any American Native population against the European invaders. Even after the Spaniards settled parts of the Southwest, travelers would take great pains, going hundreds of miles out of their way to avoid crossing the dangerous plains.

30. What is meant by the Four Corners and why was it important for the early Americans?

The point where four states meet, Arizona, Colorado, Utah and New Mexico, is known today as The Four Corners. Extending east from the Arizona border into New Mexico as far as Los Alamos and extending south from the Colorado border into New Mexico as far as Albuquerque is known as the land of the Anasazi.

31. How long had the Anasazi occupied this territory?

Evidence of their presence goes back to about 5,000 years before the Christian era.

32. What skills did these tribes possess?

These people could build and sustain fire and gather seeds, nuts and fruit. Building permanent dwellings allowed them to cultivate the soil near their villages. Their crops were corn, squash and beans. They learned the art of saving what they could not eat immediately in woven containers. Later they learned how to make pottery for carrying and preserving their water. It is relatively easy to date their accomplishments.

33. History tells us that the Anasazi abandoned this area. Why was that?

We are unable to know with certainty their reasons for abandoning these settlements. It could have been that the game they relied on was depleted or the water supply had run out.

34. What is the Bandelier National Monument?

This site is named after Adolph Bandelier, a Swiss ethnologist. It is in the heart of the Frijoles Canyon, not far from present-day Los Alamos. It is here that Bandelier made an in-depth study of the Anasazi.

35. Did Bandelier have an opinion why the Anasazi left their settlements to go south?

He believed that the drought of the late 13th Century forced them to seek a water supply on the banks of the upper Rio Grande Valley.

36. Where did the Anasazi settle?

They settled on the Pararito Plateau where they constructed intricate dwellings in the soft volcanic ash on the sides of the canyon.

37. What name did the Spaniards use in referring to the Anasazi?

The Spaniards called the Anasazi "Pueblo Indians" because they built their dwellings in the form of villages and cultivated their crops, quite different from the nomad tribes who built no permanent dwellings.

38. Why were the caves of the Anasazi so difficult to reach?

Entering these dwellings required considerable climbing, which only primates can do, thus protecting themselves from the dangerous carnivores.

39. What did historians learn about the Anasazi long after their disappearance?

Evidence remained long after the disappearance of these people that they chipped stones into hunting weapons; they preserved food supplies in baskets they made for this purpose and they protected their feet by wearing leather coverings. These Pueblo Indians were farmers, hunters and gatherers and they enjoyed a communal life rich in spiritual values. Bandelier wanted to study these interesting people so he lived in a kiva, examined hundreds of ruins and wrote numerous scientific papers. He published a fictionalized account of the inhabitants of Frijoles Canyon called *The Delight Makers* in 1890.

40. What reputation did the Apache tribes have in the Southwest?

The Apache, a nomadic tribe, earned for themselves the reputation for being particularly savage in their raids of the Pueblo Indians and the Spanish settlers in the Southwest.

41. Where did the Apache originate?

The Apache originally migrated to the Southwest from northwestern Canada and Alaska, where Athabascan tribes, speaking closely related languages still live today.

42. How did the Apache differ from the Pueblo Indians?

Unlike the Pueblo Indians, the Apache grew no crops and built no permanent dwellings.

43. What did the different Apache names mean?

The Apache had names, which described their main occupations. For example, the Mescalero Apache were so named because they were makers of mescal, which is taken from that desert plant. It belongs to the agave family and is used as a beverage and for food.

44. Who were the Jicarilla Apache?

The Jicarilla Apache were basket makers—sometimes described as indolent and unwilling to meet confrontation. They were driven from their homeland by the war-like Comanche and retreated into the mountains of Northern New Mexico.

45. What marked the end of the Apache warring lifestyle?

After many years of war and the defeat of their great leader Geronimo, the Apache were confined to reservations, putting an end to their way of life.

46. Where did the Comanche come from?

The Comanche migrated to New Mexico from the basin and mountain ranges of the Rockies.

47. What happened to the famous Pecos Annual Fair?

The annual fair in Pecos had become an important meeting place for various Indian tribes and Spaniards alike. The Comanche put an end to the lucrative trade at Pecos with a bloody raid. Jicarilla Apache fled from the warring Comanche and the trade at Pecos fell off.

48. What was the main purpose of the Comanche raids?

Most of the raids on the Pueblo Indians were to acquire horses. During one such raid on the Pecos Indians, the Comanche encountered Spanish troops from Santa Fe and fought a fierce battle with them. That day nine soldiers were killed. It was considered a great defeat for the Spanish.

49. Who were the Navaho?

The Navaho were an important sub-group of the Apache that dominated western New Mexico for centuries. They were considered Athabascans because of their linguistic origins.

50. Where did the Athabascans originate?

The Athabascans traveled south originally from Alaska and northern Canada and first encountered the Anasazi in The Four Corners area.

51. How did the Navaho tribe develop independently?

The Navaho tribe developed a culture of its own. It has been long considered that the Athabascans who adopted the Pueblo ways became Navaho. Those who preferred to continue the wild life of raiding, stealing and killing became the true Apache.

52. How did the arrival of the Spaniards affect the Navaho people?

Before the arrival of the Spaniards, there was an extensive trade existing among the various tribes. Hides, dried meat and tallow were exchanged for maize and cotton blankets of the more sedentary Indians. With the arrival of the Spaniards, a new element was introduced—the desire to impose a religion and a way of life on others.

53. What was the reaction of the Navaho to the religion of the Spanish?

The mind of the Navaho Indian, politically naïve and untutored in European Catholicism, could not grasp the subtleties of the messages brought by the Spanish friars. The freedom-loving Navaho were at constant odds with the Spaniards.

54. How did the Navaho Tribe react to the lifestyle of the Pueblo Indians and to the Spaniards?

While accepting some of the habits of the Pueblo Indians, they preferred their nomad existence, continued to raid and were even guilty of slaving against their enemy tribes. They could be just as brutal as the Spaniards. Author Douglas Preston writes: "At one point, a group of Navaho came into Taos with some Pawnee boys captured on the plains. When they found the boys couldn't be sold, they decapitated them and left."

55. What kind of houses did the Navaho provide for themselves?

The dwellings of the Navaho were the hogans built of wood and stone and covered with earth. They looked like beehives and still can be seen along the landscape of western New Mexico.

56. How did the Navaho compare to other nomadic tribes?

Of all the nomadic people, they had perhaps attained the highest degree of civilization. Much later it was the Navaho who encouraged the Pueblo Indians to revolt against the Spaniards in 1680 and collaborated with them in the uprising.

57. Which term is more appropriate, Native American or Indian?

Both terms are readily accepted by the early people of Santa Fe and its region. The Native Americans still populate much of New Mexico and the Southwest. Some would argue that the term "Native American" is inappropriate. The truth of the matter is that they were the owners of the land before the arrival of the foreigners.

58. When was the horse to make its appearance in the Southwest?

Although the horse existed in North America (we know this from skeletal remains) and probably came over the ice bridge from Asia, the people of the Southwest did not know of it until the arrival of Coronado in 1540. Fossil remains indicate that horses roamed both North and South America but disappeared long before the 1400s.

59. How important was the horse to the Plains Indians?

We know how very important the arrival of the horse was to the Plains Indians. So important was the horse to the Plains Indians that the anthropologists have named the period from 1540–1880s—the "Horse-Culture Period."

60. Was the horse as important to the Pueblo Indians?

As the Pueblo Indians learned the usefulness of this extraordinary animal, they began to raise large herds and started selling and trading them to other Indians such as the Kiowa and Comanche. When the Apache, along with the other nomad tribes, acquired this extraordinary animal, the danger to settled Indian populations and the white man became acute.

3

The Early Spaniards

61. What were the origins of Spanish exploration in the Americas?

To trace the influence of Spain in the "New World," we should look first at the exploration by Christopher Columbus of the Americas under the combined houses of Aragon and Castile. In the wake of Columbus's discovery, the Spanish invaded, explored and conquered much of the Western Hemisphere.

62. What effect did the Spaniards have on the people of Mexico?

When the Spaniards arrived in Mexico in 1492, the population of that country was about 25 million. That population dropped to 6 million in 1548 and by the end of the century was only 1,350,000 of whom one hundred thousand were Spaniards. These figures speak for the ruthlessness of the invaders in the New World and their propensity of spreading fatal disease among the natives.

63. Were the Mexicans able to hold their own against the Spanish invaders?

In battle, the superiority of the Spaniards was incontestable. Their weapons included steel swords and explosives. They presented a formidable sight in their gleaming armor astride animals unknown to the natives—horses.

64. What were the driving forces of the Spanish exploration and control?

These conquerors believed that they had been given a mission by God to take dominion over all the infidels. Cynics will say that under the guise of bringing Christianity to the natives, the invaders plundered the native people of all the wealth they possessed—their gold and silver.

65. When did the quest for riches in the new world reach its feverish level?

With the great success in finding enormous wealth in Mexico in 1521, the thirst for these precious metals reached a feverish level. In 1530, Alvar Nunez Cabeza de Vaca reported, after his travels throughout the Southwest, seeing cities of gold. Perhaps what he saw were huts built of mud and straw, which glimmered in the sunlight. Cabeza de Vaca told of his adventures, which began in 1527 when he and six hundred men left Spain in five vessels and landed near Tampa Bay in western Florida.

66. What were the goals and difficulties that Cabeza de Vaca encountered during his 1527 voyage to the coast of western Florida?

The expedition had only one goal—the seeking of gold. The Spaniards found little to eat and were poorly prepared for an extended search. The men became greatly weakened, suffering from malaria. All they could find to eat were oysters. In desperation, they killed and ate their horses.

67. What miscalculations did the explorers make concerning distances in the new world?

They believed that Mexico was immediately adjacent to Florida and they traveled along the Gulf Coast expecting a relatively short journey. In a small boat, Cabeza de Vaca and a few men drifted aimlessly for days until they came ashore on a barrier island, now believed to be Galveston Island, Texas.

68. During the travels of Cabeza de Vaca, a Moor played an important role. What was it?

The writings of Cabeza de Vaca tell of a black Moorish slave named Esteban one of the few survivors with himself to endure more than a year of captivity among a local tribe of Indians. Upon relating, to the Spanish viceroy in Mexico, the years of wandering through the Southwest, much of the time with his companion Esteban, Cabeza de Vaca particularly excited the viceroy's interest with the mention of great cities to the north and the elaborately dressed women wearing jewelry. The viceroy asked him to go back to lead a reconnaissance party but Cabeza de Vaca declined; the African, Esteban, however, agreed to go.

69. Who was Marcos de Niza and what role did he have in the exploration of the Southwest?

In 1538, the Spanish viceroy in Mexico, Antonio Mendoza, made a Franciscan priest, Marcos de Niza, the leader in a reconnaissance of the lands north of Mexico. Marcos de Niza immediately put Esteban in charge of an advanced party of Aztecs. Esteban had no sooner entered the first of the Seven Cities, than he and almost all of his men were slain by arrows. Within a year, the priest returned to Mexico City claiming to have seen a large city that the Zuni Indians called Cibolo. This city was supposed to be only one of seven cities of gold.

70. What brought Francisco Vazquez de Coronado into the exploration of the Southwest?

Marcos de Niza's reports ignited the lust for gold even more so. Viceroy Mendoza was so impressed he wanted to lead an expedition himself— perhaps to rival De Soto's successes in Florida. Instead, he commissioned a young nobleman by the name of Francisco Vazquez de Coronado—just thirty years old. In February of 1540, Coronado departed the town of Compostela with about three hundred soldiers, a few Franciscans, more than a thousand Indian slaves and more than fifteen hundred horses and pack animals on his way into the new territory.

71. How did Coronado plan to explore the Southwest and beyond?

Establishing a base among the Pueblo villages along the Rio Grande, Coronado explored parts of present-day Arizona, New Mexico, Texas, Oklahoma and Kansas. Why did he venture into the plains? A man called the "Turk," whose reasons are unclear, had lied to him about the existence of the Cities of Gold. Perhaps it was to lose the Spaniards in the wilderness where there was insufficient food and little water. Jaramillo (recorder of the journey) wrote: "We understood, however, that he (the Turk) was leading us away from the route we ought to follow...so we would eat up all the food... and become weak."

72. What terminated Coronado's exploration of this area?

It was not until springtime of 1542 that Coronado made his way back to Mexico, having failed in his mission of procuring gold for his king. Coronado realized that Friar Marcos had lied about the gold. With each step of this journey, he had been assured, by those closest to him that the Cities of Gold were just over the horizon. The Spaniards garroted the Turk for his treachery and left him where he fell. The great riches of Mexico and Peru had not materialized in this barren country.

73. How did Coronado express himself to the King of Spain regarding the hardships of his travels through the Southwest?

In a letter to the king, he wrote: "...with only thirty horsemen whom I took for my escort, I traveled forty-two days, living all this while solely on the flesh of the bulls and cows which we killed and going many days without water, and cooking the food with cow dung, because there is not any kind of wood in all these plains."

74. How did the soldiers of Coronado fare against the Indians?

History bears out that, although Coronado's men were greatly outnumbered, they inflicted grave damage on the Pueblo Indians whenever these native people refused to do the bidding of the invaders.

75. What was Coronado's legacy for his extensive travel and hardships?

A protégé of Mendoza, Coronado wanted more than monetary wealth for himself. He wanted to be hailed as a great conqueror, a hero for the Spanish people. It was, thanks to the efforts of Coronado and his men that new maps were drawn of the regions, which greatly assisted those who followed him. Of the Europeans, it was he who learned first that California was not an island; it was he who first saw the Rocky Mountains and ventured into the Great Plains.

76. What was the immediate result of Coronado's exploration?

For an entire generation, no further expeditions were made into New Mexico. Fray Agustin Rodriquez led a group of missionaries into New Mexico in 1581 but they were all killed. In 1590, Gaspar Castaño led an unauthorized expedition into New Mexico but was chased by the Spanish army and imprisoned. A street in historic Santa Fe is named after him—Don Gaspar.

4

Religion and Myth in the 17th Century

77. How did the occupying Spaniards view the religious practices of the natives?

One can easily understand but not so easily condone the arrogance of the conquering Spaniards in matters of religion. Had they not been taught that the Holy Catholic Church was the true Church and all other religions were false? They treated the natives with disdain.

78. Why did the Franciscan friars not respect the religious beliefs of the natives?

Franciscan friars who accompanied the soldiers maintained that these natives were nothing but beasts because they had not had the sacrament of baptism. It was the duty of the Church to bring the blessings of Christianity to these lost souls.

79. Why was it so difficult for the Spaniards to understand the religious beliefs of the tribes?

It would take centuries of enlightenment to understand that praying in a dance is no different than praying on one's knees; that seeking help from the earth mother was no different than praying to the Virgin. It would take centuries of enlightenment to want to understand and value the religious beliefs of the natives.

80. What happened to those tribe members who resisted the teachings of the friars?

Those who would not submit to the holy sacraments were put to death.

81. What had the friars not understood about the spiritual beliefs of the natives?

If the Franciscan friars could have understood the Indians, they would have learned that the reverence they held for animals was respect for what that animal could teach. The rattlesnake, for example, could teach the natives how to move quietly through the grass and strike their prey without being heard. The power of the bird was that it could soar high above the canyons in minutes while it took man hours and perhaps days to cover the same distance. It was to the bird that they asked help to attain these powers.

82. How did the nudity of Indians confuse and disturb the church members?

The Spaniards viewed the Indians' frank and totally unconscious nudity and their phallic worship to be depraved. One can remember that in pre-Christian Pompeii, the concern with fertility led the inhabitants to use the phallus as a token of strength. Much of what we marvel at today in Pompeii was covered up by volcanic ash for centuries and discovered only at a time when we, through understanding, could view such art with objective interest.

83. How did the natives preserve their beliefs in view of Spanish hostility?

Because the Franciscans would not understand, the natives accepted the dictates of the Catholic Church but went underground and kept their own beliefs in secret. The kiva was a place of reflection and prayer. Kivas were dug deep within the earth in circular shapes, far from critical eyes. The Spaniards who saw them thought they were used for cooking and named them "estufas" or stoves. It was later that they learned that this was a holy place where the elders of the community gathered to seek help in their prayers for decisions they were contemplating.

84. How did the religious beliefs of the Europeans differ from those of the Indians?

Through the development of science, the white man learned what god was not. Unlike the Greeks and Romans, he no longer worshiped the sea, the sun or the wind. The Indian, however, had a complete and personal relationship with nature and manifested his religious beliefs through prayers, dances and songs. He who seemed to be able to interpret the will of the gods was the Shaman. These men had a special relationship with the gods, wore distinctive outerwear, feathers and masks to emphasize their importance. Where confusion existed, they brought clarity; they were the decision makers. Who, indeed, would question the man so close to the gods? They were able by some mystic power within themselves to create "good" medicine and dispel "bad" medicine.

85. What role does symbolism play?

Symbolism plays an important part in all religions. Christians have the Cross, a symbol of the sacrificing of life and its resurrection for the faithful. Catholics take the Host into their mouths at Holy Communion symbolic of eating the body of Christ and use the Rosary Beads in prayer. The Shaman wears the mask of the deity he is communicating with to personify this deity. The native uses the Pahos, or prayer stick, often made up of eagle feathers to symbolize that, as the eagle soars into the eye of the sun, so may his prayers ascend to the Divine Ones.

86. Were the Indians superstitious?

Witchcraft was universal among the Indian tribes and superstition a prime factor in their lives. Whatever the untutored mind did not understand was associated with some mystical power.

87. Why were mothers especially fearful of witches?

Young mothers were especially vulnerable to witches because they were known to be baby snatchers. Mothers were especially solicitous of their infants. They would cover their children's heads and faces whenever they came into the presence of a witch.

88. Why were the Indians fearful of showing ownership of nice things?

The Indians would be careful not to be ostentatious of ownership of any beautiful string of beads or brightly colored blanket for fear that they might cause a witch to be jealous of them.

89. What were the special powers of the witches and their curses?

Deformity was always the result of a curse. If a dead cat were to be thrown near a person, that person would often be seized with paralysis. Witches thrived in darkness and shadows. They could assume the shape of animals and enter the very smallest spaces. They could travel great distances in the blink of an eye.

90. What are the origins of religious self-flagellation?

Inflicting pain upon ones own body is not strictly a peculiarity of early Christians imitating the passion of Jesus Christ. The ancient Egyptians whipped themselves in honor of Isis. Likewise evidence of self-flagellation was witnessed in Sparta.

91. What is the history of this kind of self-abuse in Spain?

The Order of Los Hermanos Penitentes was founded in Spain over 300 years ago, in direct disobedience of the papal bull, which prohibited this activity.

92. Were there similar practices among the American Indians?

The Spanish conquistadors upon arriving in New Mexico found traces of a similar custom. Author Charles F. Lummis writes: "It is interesting to note that tribal penance, vicariously done, has been a custom among Pueblo Indians from time immemorial, and still is observed. Twice a year, in each of the nineteen now-inhabited pueblos, a penitential fast of four days is kept... In Isleta six men and six women are selected to expiate for the sins of the whole pueblo." All the Pueblo tribes had their professional penitents. Some inflicted pain on themselves with the thorns of the cactus.

93. What was the practice of the Mexicans in this regard?

It was the Mexicans in the Southwest who brought this activity to levels that resulted in condemnation. They would whip themselves with iron nails, carry wooden crosses to exhaustion and allow themselves to be crucified. It may not be overstated to say that these penitents, by inflicting great pain on themselves and then denying the existence of this pain, were able to reach high levels of spiritual bliss.

94. What role did the taboos play?

Taboos play a role in many religions. Jews, for example, will not mix milk dishes with meat dishes. Catholics, for centuries, would not eat meat on Fridays or have food in their stomachs when they took Holy Communion. Many taboos have their origin in sensible customs—do not eat in a stranger's house, do not fall asleep in an unfamiliar place. Among the Zunis of New Mexico, there are those who may never eat the flesh of a badger, bear of coyote. To the Navaho, fish, ducks, snakes and rabbits are taboo.

95. How do the faithful perceive the relative power of their gods?

The relative power of the gods plays an important role. In prayer, one cannot approach an all-powerful god directly but only through the good graces of a less powerful god. Catholics pray to their favorite saints to intercede with the Virgin for help with their prayers. When the Pueblo Indians witnessed the arrival of the Spanish soldiers and priests along the Camino Real and saw above them the dark clouds of rain, they believed that the gods of these people had to be more powerful than their own gods. For hadn't the Indians been praying for rain during many months of drought and had no success while these strangers brought the rain with them?

5

Don Juan de Oñate

96. When the Spaniards in New Spain (Mexico) were ready for a continuation of their exploration, to whom did they turn?

By 1595, the disappointments of Viceroy Mendoza and Coronado may have been forgotten. A new viceroy for the crown—Luis de Velasco signed a contract with a wealthy man for the occupation and colonization of the land that would be called "New Mexico." This was Don Juan de Oñate.

97. Who was this man and how did he convince the viceroy of his worth?

Oñate was persistent in his urgings and a good friend of the viceroy but perhaps not the best person for this task. Unlike his predecessors who traveled north from Mexico City to pillage whatever wealth they could, Oñate was a businessman, made wealthy from the silver mining in Zacatecas. He was married to Isabel de Tolosa Cortes Moctezuma, the granddaughter of Hernan Cortez and the great granddaughter of Moctezuma.

98. What were the terms of his commission?

Oñate would bear the cost of the expedition and by contract would receive the title of governor and enjoy a share of the profits this new kingdom would produce. He would be paid a salary of 6,000 ducats a year and have unlimited power, reporting only to the Council of the Indies in Spain.

99. What red tape did Oñate encounter?

For many weeks he camped along the banks of the Rio Concho in what is now northern Mexico, and waited for the political wrangling to cease so that he could have permission to head north. All the time, he spent large sums of his own money to maintain the men in arms and the other colonists.

100. When was he finally given permission to begin his journey?

Finally in 1598, he set forth, with about 130 soldier-settlers, their wives, children and servants and about eight priests and about eighty wagons. This brought the total number of people to about 500. With great difficulty, the caravan crossed the arid Mexican desert. Food was scarce and water was difficult to find. One expeditionary member, poet-soldier Gaspar Perez de Villagra wrote: "Two of the thirst-crazed horses" when they finally reached the banks of the Rio Grande, "drank so much that their bellies burst open."

101. What unusual way did Oñate claim the new territory for the Spanish crown?

After passing the spot that was later named "El Paso," Oñate proclaimed Spanish dominion over the new land and all its inhabitants, "from the leaves of the trees in the forests to the stones and sands of the river."

102. What historical importance does the town of Socorro have?

Oñate's party traveled north over the dry stretch where the Rio Grande disappeared underground and was given food and drink in a village, which in gratitude he named "Socorro," meaning "help" in Spanish. Again Perez de Villagra wrote: "…The light party arrived at the pueblo of Teypana on June 14, 1598 where they received a most gracious welcome. Chief Letoc was not only generous with his corn, but he also provided the Spaniards with valuable information about the land and the people ahead."

103. Where did Oñate settle at the end of his journey?

North of present-day Santa Fe, near what is now the town of Espanola, Oñate made his headquarters in the Tewa Pueblo of San Juan, chasing the natives from their lodgings. Oñate ordered the construction of St. Gabriel, New Mexico's first capital.

104. How large was the caravan that arrived at this destination?

This caravan was made up of about eighty-five wagons, extending several miles long with its livestock numbering in the thousands.

105. Did Oñate have personal reasons for taking on this exploration of the Southwest?

Although the main purpose for establishing a governor for New Mexico was the pacification and Christianization of the Indians, Oñate had a hidden agenda of seeking out any silver mines he could find. He had brought along heavy mining tools and supplies for that purpose.

106. From our present-day perspective, what can we not understand about the attitude of the Spanish settlers?

It can be disputed that Oñate had the best interests of New Spain and the king of Spain at heart. He may have had good intentions of showing the natives kindness but it is difficult for us to understand fully the mentality of the armed men who invaded New Mexico. To enter a land where tribes of people lived, hunted and tilled the earth and to claim everything in view for the Spanish Crown is a bit difficult for us to accept.

107. What other indignities were forced on the natives?

Not only did the Spaniards claim the land but they also forced the natives to feed their armies and kneel to an unknown god.

108. How does history view the conquest of the Southwest by Oñate?

Because of his preoccupation with finding silver mines and his need for approval from the viceroy, Oñate became an absent leader, traveling as far as the Gulf of California and into present-day Kansas. He all but ignored the hardships of the settlers, many of whom deserted the settlement and returned to Mexico. During these first years, many letters of complaint were sent to the viceroy, which were balanced by the optimism Oñate displayed in his own reports of impending success of finding riches. The 46-year-old Oñate may have lacked maturity to be a benevolent statesman. Perhaps he was no more brutal or greedy than his predecessors but he has been perceived as such.

109. What major event had convinced Oñate of the dangerous intent of the natives?

Perhaps one of the most salient episodes is that of the destruction of Acoma, west of present-day Albuquerque. On top of a 400-foot high mesa, protected on all sides by steep cliffs, the Pueblo of Acoma stood since about 1075. The Acoma warriors were greatly feared by the surrounding pueblos. When Don Juan de Oñate went to Acoma to receive a new allegiance from these proud people, he did not understand the resentment they felt. The natives gave their oath and invited Oñate to visit one of their underground ceremonial chambers called "kivas." Something made Oñate hesitate and refuse to descend which may have saved his life.

110. What act of brutality did the Indians of Acoma commit against the Spaniards?

A few weeks after Oñate's close call with death, one of Oñate's closest officers, Juan de Zaldivar with thirty men stopped by the pueblo and was invited in by the natives. Foolishly the Spaniards allowed themselves to be separated and all but four of them were brutally killed. Those who escaped did so by throwing themselves off the mesa. Juan de Zaldivar was not one of the survivors. When these four returned to report the massacre to Oñate, the governor weighed his options but realized that he could not let this revolt stand without punishment for fear it would encourage other pueblos to do the same.

111. How did Oñate retaliate?

With the approval of the counsel of the friars, Oñate sent Juan de Zaldivar's brother, Vicente with seventy men to punish the Acomese. The accounts of the battle on top of the mesa are disputed by several sources but what is clear is that the Spaniards, greatly outnumbered, waged a bloody battle and forced the natives to surrender. At any rate, it was a bloody slaughter. The captives, numbering perhaps 80 men and 500 women and children were returned to San Juan where a "trial" ensued. Oñate sentenced all the captives between the ages of 12 and 25 to twenty years of personal servitude and he condemned males older than 25 to have one foot severed. In Renaissance

Europe, this was not an uncommon punishment. As a lesson to others who might be tempted to defy the Crown, Oñate carried out the mutilations in public.

112. What was the population of Acoma at the time of this battle?

There seems to be controversy as to the size of the population of Acoma at this time. In Oñate's report, he estimated the population to be about 3,000. Adolph Bandelier estimated the population to have been about 1,000.

113. What is Oñate's legacy?

Ten years after he departed for his governorship in New Mexico, Oñate was depleted of his money, reviled by his followers and accused of heinous crimes. He took it upon himself to resign. In his own defense, Oñate wrote: "Unable to overcome my zeal and good purpose, the devil has exhausted my resources and I find myself unable to explore any further at a moment when the reports are most promising and encouraging." The first governor of New Mexico and colonizer of the land north of Mexico is remembered in history as something less than a conquistador. He is remembered by many for his brutality and greed.

6

Don Pedro de Peralta

114. What was the growing attitude about continuing the Spanish occupation of New Mexico?

At about the time when Jamestown, Virginia was being established, King Philip III of Spain was considering vacating the province of New Mexico. The costs for maintaining settlements there were enormous.

115. Why was the king persuaded to reconsider his attitude?

The year was 1608. The king was dissuaded by his viceroy in Mexico who reported that more than 7,000 natives had been converted to Christianity and their souls would indeed be in jeopardy without the continued blessings of holy sacraments.

116. Who followed Oñate as the new Governor of New Mexico?

In 1609, the king appointed Don Pedro de Peralta to be the new governor. Many consider Peralta to be the first governor of New Mexico, as they clearly write-off Oñate as a spoiler and a cruel and corrupt businessman. The first capital, nevertheless, had been established on the Chama River where Oñate built San Gabriel. When Peralta was selected to become the governor of New Mexico, he was told to move the capital to a more central place, where he would not displace any native settlements.

117. Where did Peralta build his capital?

The Royal City of the Holy Faith or Santa Fe was established on the banks of a full-flowing river that was to take the name of the city.

118. To whom was Santa Fe dedicated?

The city was dedicated to its patron saint—San Francisco d'Assisi.

119. Why was the capital called Santa Fe?

Under the combined rule of Ferdinand and Isabella in 1492, another Santa Fe had been built beside the city of Granada, Spain. Granada was the last Moorish stronghold remaining as the Christians drove the Moors from the peninsula. Unwilling to destroy the city because of its marvelous architecture, the Catholic Monarchs decided to use this Santa Fe de Granada to establish a siege to force out the Moors. It worked. Now the city of Santa Fe, New Mexico would have a similar role—displace or convert the pagans.

120. Had Indians ever lived on the site selected by Peralta?

Although no natives lived on the site selected by Peralta for the city, ancestors of the Pueblo Indians populated this site between 3,000 B.C and 600 A.D. Perhaps they left this site in search of more abundant water supplies.

121. Who built the first Plaza, which we have admired for more than four hundred years?

It is to Peralta that we owe our thanks for the Plaza, which extended originally up to the Cathedral and the Palace of Governors, constructed in 1610–1612. The Palace is today the oldest government building in the United States.

122. What was the design of the Plaza?

The plaza was similar in design to about 11,000 other Spanish plazas throughout the Americas as ordered by a decree of the Law of the Indies. Its recommended dimensions were 600 feet by 400 feet and that eight streets were to run from it—two from each corner and one from the center of each long side. In addition to serving as a meeting place for the citizens of the city, the plaza was used by the army as a drill field for the soldiers.

123. What other function did the Plaza have?

The social life of the city would revolve around the plaza. It may be difficult to imagine, seeing the Plaza today, that at various times it was a dusty field, turning to mud in the winter, an extension of a local farm and covered with cornstalks or a grazing field for livestock.

124. How does the building of Santa Fe compare in time to the arrival of the Pilgrims on the East Coast?

As a point of comparison, Santa Fe was founded ten years before the Pilgrims landed on Plymouth Rock and is the oldest capital in the nation. Curiously having the oldest capital, New Mexico was one of the last states to be accepted into the Union.

125. What was the reason for this long delay?

This was mostly due to the attitude of Congress that believed the Spanish language and culture of New Mexico were definitely non-American. There was also the matter of Congress being unwilling to upset the balance of "slave" versus "free" states that kept New Mexico out of consideration. It was only when the xenophobia subsided a bit that New Mexico was admitted to the Union as the 47th State in 1912.

126. What is significant about the church San Miguel in Santa Fe?

At the high point of the city, beyond the river on the southeast side was the Barrio de Analco, which means "neighborhood on the other side." This was where the Mexican slaves who accompanied Peralta to Santa Fe were to be housed in their own neighborhood. For purposes of their own worship, a church was built in 1610. This church, named "San Miguel," was built on the ruins of an old native kiva. For that reason, San Miguel is said to have the oldest church foundations in the United States.

127. What measures were taken to assure that the Indians would be treated with more respect than they had been under Oñate?

Sensitive about all the complaints that had been made about Oñate, the

Viceroy Don Luis de Velasco gave specific orders to Peralta in dealing with the natives: "Inasmuch as it has been reported that the tribute levied on the natives is excessive, and that it is collected with much vexation and trouble to them, we charge the governor to take suitable measures in this matter, proceeding in such a way as to relieve and satisfy the royal conscience." There was to be a kinder and gentler IRS.

128. How did the viceroy address the matter of security?

The viceroy went on to tell Peralta that the security of the settlers was foremost and that any trouble with the Indians should be handled peacefully if possible but by force if necessary.

129. How successful were the first years of Peralta's administration?

During a time of relative peace with the Pueblo Indians, the community was caught in an internal conflict between the civil authority of the governor and the religious authority of the Church. It was also a time of great construction. Peralta occupied himself with the building of the Palace of the Governors while the Franciscan prelate of the New Mexico Missions, Alonso de Peinado, supervised the building of a church for Santa Fe.

130. Is this the church we presently see in Santa Fe?

No, by 1640, the church had collapsed—it was constructed of mud mortar. It was not until two hundred years later that a strongly-built cathedral, Saint Francis, would appear on the same site.

131. What was the design of the Palace of the Governors?

The Palace of the Governors, more solidly built than the church constructed at the same time, was designed in the Spanish Colonial Style—one story with an overhanging portico to provide shade from the sun and protection from the rains. The flat roof was supported by exposed vigas. The walls were in most places three feet thick, which kept the Palace cool in the summer and warm in the winter.

132. In addition to thick walls, what other provisions for security were planned in the design?

The windows in the first structure were narrow to protect the inhabitants from having more than one invader enter at a time, in the event of an assault.

133. Was glass available for the windows?

There was no glass for the windows at first but in time sheets of mica were used to allow the rays of sunlight to enter.

134. Is the Palace of the Governors now as it was in the original design?

Although viewing the Palace today, we have a good idea of the original structure; the Palace of 1612 was larger. The Palace was to change in design many times over the following centuries.

135. What were some of the design changes that were made over the years?

In 1772, for example, the Palace was modified as a new presidio with an open rectangle to accommodate a garrison of troops, which gave it the air of a military installation. In 1850 a territorial style porch was added. A hard stucco façade was added in 1872. U.S. Marshall John Sherman ordered a complete remodeling of the Palace's façade in 1877. A plank sidewalk was added; the porch posts were wrapped in elaborate moldings and each capped with a heavy cornice.

136. When did the Palace receive official status?

In 1909, the New Mexico legislature offered the Palace as an official headquarters building with an annual appropriation of $5,000. The newspaper, *The Santa Fe New Mexican* called the establishing of a museum in the Palace a magnificent idea. It would not be just of local interest but national and even international interest.

137. What caused the Palace to undergo a radical change in design?

As a result of the arrival of the railway to New Mexico in 1878, tourism increased and with it a sense of nostalgia for the past. It was this sentiment that moved architect and photographer Jesse Nusbaum in 1912 to return the Palace to the style he believed it had originally been. Gone was the Greek Revival Style porch and with it went the Victorian colonnade.

138. Why is the Palace of the Governors now a museum instead of just an historic building?

Today, the Palace of the Governors as a museum is or should be on everyone's must-see list. Under the portal, on most days, one can see native Pueblo Indian vendors. In the late 1970s, a graduate student in law protested that it was racial discrimination to allow only Pueblo Indians to display their wares in front of the Palace. He filed a lawsuit when he could not display his jewelry there. By making the Indians an integral part of the museum, the director managed to defeat the lawsuit.

139. Who selects the Indians to display their wares each day?

Each day the Indians take part in a lottery to determine who will have the opportunity to display their wares that day, since there are many more artisans than spaces in front of the museum.

7

Church and State

140. What change in the administration of the church brought about the beginning of conflict with the civil authorities?

Often bad chemistry between individuals is enough to spark serious discord. So it was when in late summer of 1612 a new prelate was appointed to replace Friar Peinado. From Mexico City came Friar Isidro Ordonez with ideas quite firm about his role in the society of Santa Fe. Joseph Sanchez writes: "Everyone knew Friar Ordonez's presence spelled trouble. When Governor Peralta heard Ordonez had replaced Peinado, he was heard to exclaim, 'Would to God the devil were coming instead of that friar!'"

141. What was known about Ordonez?

Ordonez was not a stranger to Santa Fe. He had served under Oñate and was hated by many. When Ordonez took it upon himself to order tribute collectors to return to Santa Fe from Taos, after Peralta had ordered them there, a serious break took place between them.

142. What happened to create such a rift?

The break between Friar Ordonez and Governor Peralta occurred in May 1613, when the prelate interfered with the governor's privileged functions to collect the annual tribute of corn and blankets from the pueblos. As the tribute collectors bound for Taos went past Nambe Pueblo, north of Santa Fe, Ordonez intercepted them, and under threat of excommunication, ordered them to return to the village to hear mass, for the Feast of the Pentecost was at hand. Upon their return, Captain Pedro Ruiz, leader of the tribute collectors, reported to the governor, who ordered them back on the trail.

143. How did this dispute escalate?

Ordonez would not accept the authority of the governor or at least considered that authority subordinate to his own. Ordonez threatened the governor with excommunication unless he ordered the tribute collectors to return. Peralta refused which initiated a series of acts—including Ordonez putting a letter of excommunication on the door of the church, and throwing the governor's chair out of the church. Insults following insults, the drawing of arms and the accidental wounding of a priest brought the fever of discord to an uncontrollable level. Angered, Ordonez mounted the pulpit and spoke clearly to the congregation: "Do not be deceived. Let no one persuade himself with vain words that I do not have the same power and authority that the Pope in Rome has, or that if his Holiness were here in New Mexico, he could do more than I. Believe you that I can arrest, cast into irons, and punish as seems fitting to me any person without exception who is not obedient to the commandments of the church or mine."

144. What were the results of this action by the church?

It may be difficult to understand the great power of the Catholic Church from our present-day perspective. As result of his insults against the church, Peralta was taken prisoner as he was making his way south. He was held in a cell for eight months before he escaped. The governor was weak and tired and attempted to hide but was found by Ordonez's men. He was imprisoned for another year when news came from Mexico City that a new governor been named.

145. What church movement did this action of Ordonez provoke?

With the establishment of the Inquisition in New Mexico in 1626, a series of investigations took place, which revealed much abuse on the part of the civil government but also abuse among the clergy. The first agent of the Inquisition, Fray Alonso de Benevides, proved to be "a model of reason and moderation." Because of his correspondence and his book, *Memorial*, we have such a good knowledge of life in Santa Fe at that period. From his writings we read: "They (the congregation) lacked a church, as their first one had collapsed. I built a very fine church for them, at which they, their wives, and children personally aided me considerably by carrying the materials and helping to build the walls with their own hands."

8

The Pueblo Revolt

146. In subsequent years, what further action did the Spanish Inquisition take?

As we have seen by the discord and the constant struggle for power between the civil and religious leaders, the Spanish community was, in the long run, the loser. The Spanish Inquisition continued to thrive in Santa Fe. The Holy Office accused more than one governor of crimes. Although Peralta was returned to Mexico in shame, he was later exonerated and Ordonez was reprimanded for his handling of the matter. Don Fernando Lopez de Mendizabal, governor of New Mexico (1656–1661), was arrested, imprisoned and died in custody but was later absolved of his "crimes" by the Inquisition. It did not take much of an accusation on the part of the Church to have even the highest civil authority brought down. Had not a precedent been set? Lopez de Mendizabal was accused of being a practicing Jew because he and his wife bathed on the Sabbath. The Church was eager to review all accusations, for their own edification, and often saw that neighbor would accuse neighbor of blasphemy just because of property disputes.

147. How did the Indians take advantage of the discord between church and state?

Eighty years after the Spaniards came north from Mexico to make a permanent settlement in Santa Fe, the Pueblo Indians revolted and drove them out.

148. What were some of the most important reasons for the revolt?

We have touched on some of the reasons for the anger and frustration of the Indians. They did not like being made slaves of the invaders. They did not like having to accept the religion of the Catholic Church. During the great building projects during the Peralta years, they were severely under compensated for their work. Having once believed that the gods of the

Spaniards were more powerful than their own gods, they now had second thoughts. The land was, in recent years, under a severe drought and the Christian God did not bring relief.

149. What other reasons did the Indians have for losing respect for the Spaniards?

The Indians were constantly observing the disputes among their masters and realized that it was weakness they saw not strength. The Indians lost respect for both civil and religious leaders.

150. What methods of control did the Spaniards often use?

Despite the laws that prohibited it, often their masters abused the Indian workers. To instill Christianity, the Spaniards often resorted to floggings, torture and even hanging.

151. When did this revolt begin?

In 1680, the Indians rebelled. There had been other smaller attempts but this time it was well organized. An Indian medicine man named Popé had planned for five years to bring this about. The authorities had disciplined him by public flogging but his determination was firm.

152. How did the Indians coordinate their revolt with other tribes?

From Taos to Isleta, with the exception of Santa Fe, the Indians communicated by knotted cords to indicate a timeline for the attack and slowly moved in from all sides on the capital.

153. How did the Indians show their anger against the Spaniards?

The countryside was devastated, the churches were burned and holy shrines were defiled. Homes were looted and about four hundred settlers—men, women and children, including priests were killed.

154. How quickly did the revolt progress?

The revolt began on Saturday, August 10th, on the Feast of San Lorenzo. In the early days of the revolt, the governor was not aware that anything was amiss. By August 15th, the city of Santa Fe was under siege. Refugees from the outlying areas came for protection to the Palace of the Governors. On the events of the Pueblo Revolt, David Weber writes: "Then, in a few weeks in the late summer of 1680, Pueblos destroyed the Spanish colony of New Mexico, coordinating their efforts, as they had never done before. Pueblos launched a well-planned surprise attack. From the kiva at Taos, Pueblo messengers secretly carried calendars in the form of knotted cords to participating pueblos. Each knot marked a day until the Pueblos would take up arms."

155. How effective was the Indian leader?

Unquestionably, Popé was behind the spirit and drive of this revolt. His focus was constant and his energy boundless. Those who fault him for his methods should remember our own American Revolution. We demanded freedom from the oppressor, as did the Pueblo Indians. At least 20,000 Indians pledged themselves to the revolt. The uprising was scheduled for the night of the new moon but word leaked out. Two Christian Indians at Tesuque warned the governor so the date of the revolt was moved up.

156. How prepared were the Spaniards for the Indian Revolt?

Governor Otermin was caught off guard, as were many of the three thousand Spaniards spread along the Rio Grande. The Indians killed twenty-one of the thirty-three Franciscans. Thomas James relates these events when he wrote: "Instigated by their medicine-men, the Indians were particularly vindictive in their treatment of the padres. Father Juan Jesus, the oldest priest at Jemez, was awakened in the dead of night, was dragged from his bed and made to carry the Indians. He was cast out and devoured by wolves. At Acoma, the padre was stripped naked, dragged about the streets with a rope around his neck. He was then beaten to death with clubs."

157. How did the Pueblo Indians make an attempt to end the bloodshed peacefully?

With the Indians surrounding the Palace of the Governors and cutting off the water supply, the Indians gave the governor a choice—leave peacefully and return to Mexico under a white flag of truce or be put to death. The Spaniards fought hard, managing to drive off the Pecos and the Tanos but the Indians of the north continued the siege.

158. How did the revolt finally come to an end?

Governor Otermin received two wounds, one in his face and the other in his chest. Another week passed and after trying once more to save his Palace, Governor Otermin finally surrendered. He walked out of the Palace with just under two thousand settlers and they made their way down to El Paso.

159. What did the Spaniards do to attempt a return to Santa Fe?

In 1681, Otermin received orders from the viceroy. He was to return to New Mexico to attempt to repossess it. He headed northward with a party of 147 soldiers. In a pitiful show of force, he burned what was unimportant and made a show of power without really having any. When the Pueblo Indians who had no intention of giving back what they had gained the year before faced Otermin with their own show of strength, Otermin gave up.

160. How successful was the Pueblo Revolt?

The Pueblo Revolt had been a success; the Pueblo People had won their independence—at least for the next twelve years.

161. How many Spanish governors ruled Santa Fe from its founding until the Pueblo Revolt?

Between 1610 and 1680, there had been twenty-three governors to rule New Mexico. One governor—Juan Duran de Miranda served twice, but not consecutively. At the time of the revolt in 1680, three generations of Santa Feans had been born in the city and reached adulthood there. About 87% of the people were at this time natives of the province.

162. How did the victorious Indians seek to undo the influence of the Spaniards?

As a reaction to the religion that had been imposed on them, the Indians tried to bathe and rub off the holy water with which they had been baptized. Popé declared that all marriages made under Spanish rule would be considered wrong and had to be redone according to native tradition. Popé ordered that all plant life not native to the Pueblo Indians be torn up and burned. Those horses not taken by the fleeing Spaniards were turned out and allowed to run free, much to the delight of the Apache and Comanche Indians, who were in sore need of transportation for their raiding parties.

163. How did Pedro Garcia explain the revolt to Governor Otermin?

When Otermin later interrogated a Tano Indian known as Pedro Garcia, the governor wanted to know why the Indians had rebelled. Pedro said that the Pueblos were tired of all the work they had to do for the Spaniards and the missionaries. It angered them that they did not have time to plant for themselves or to do other things they needed to do. When Governor Otermin interrogated another Indian, a Tiwa man from Alameda, the governor learned the resentment that the Indians felt was great...because the Spaniards took away their idols and forbade their sorceries and mocked their ancient customs. The governor later learned from Pueblo captives about Popé's administration of New Mexico.

164. What were Popé's orders in this regard?

"He (Popé) ordered in all the pueblos through which he passed that they instantly break up and burn the images of the holy Christ, the Virgin Mary and other saints, the crosses and everything pertaining to Christianity."

165. What do we know for certain about the self-rule of the Pueblo Indians?

There is not much reliable documentation of the years of the Pueblo rule in New Mexico. We do know that there were quarrels among the Indians when they no longer had the Spanish to subjugate them. With the Spanish gone, there was no more need among the Pueblos for unity. Popé was criticized for exhibiting some of the same traits that the Spanish governor had shown—overbearing and immovable in matters of his decisions.

166. How significant was the Pueblo Revolt in American History?

The history of the Southwest has not been of great interest to many American historians but those who are interested in the Southwest have regarded the Pueblo Revolt as a significant event. It was the only time in North America that an Indian revolt had been successful.

9

Don Diego de Vargas

167. How did the King of Spain feel about his investments in New Mexico?

Spain had lost considerable money and prestige in its occupation of New Mexico. The King of Spain, Philip III had grown tired of the drain this venture had on his treasury. He would have much preferred to spend the money on court entertainment. Unlike his formidable father, Philip II who was always in control of events, Philip III allowed his ministers to make important decisions for him especially his favorite—Francisco Gomez de Sandoval.

168. Who presented himself to the Viceroy in Mexico in order to take on the reconquest of New Mexico?

This was Don Diego de Vargas, a gentleman from an important Spanish family. He desired to undertake the reconquest of New Mexico in a peaceful campaign. Don Diego's family had distinguished itself over the years as knights and crusaders, diplomats and bishops. It is strange that this handsome, wealthy man would want to take on the hardships of life in New Mexico when he had all the advantages of a privileged existence in New Spain.

169. When did de Vargas begin his journey to Santa Fe?

The Viceroy in Mexico, Conde de Galve, tried to dissuade de Vargas from pursuing such a mission. Finally with permission of the viceroy, de Vargas made his way from Mexico up the Camino Real as his predecessors had done, over the dusty trails and up along the Rio Grande. Six months later, he arrived at his destination. It was September 1692.

170. Upon arriving at the former capital—Santa Fe, what did de Vargas do?

De Vargas led his men—soldiers and robed Franciscan friars—across the fields and plaza of the former Spanish capital and stood in front of the former Spanish palace. He gave orders to his men not to fire their weapons unless he unsheathed his sword.

171. What changes had the Pueblo Indians made to the Palace since the revolt?

The Palace of the Governors had changed considerably since being occupied by the Pueblo Indians—mostly from the Galisteo area. The Indians had built a defensive wall around the Palace, which remained in place until de Vargas' successor Governor Cubero ordered it taken down. The Indians had built several stories atop the Palace in their own style. Many Indians now lived within the walls and they watched the de Vargas procession with curiosity and some concern.

172. How did de Vargas address the Indians?

With his helmet in his hand, astride his horse, de Vargas told the Indians through an interpreter that he had come in peace; that the King of Spain forgave them for the desecration of the holy shrines, the destruction of the churches and the killing of the priests and other Spaniards. He had come to have them renew their vows of obedience to the Spanish King—Almighty God's servant on earth.

173. How did the Indians react to de Vargas?

Whether the Indians understood that this was a reconquest of New Mexico or not isn't clear but the bows that had been trained on de Vargas were lowered. De Vargas heard or thought he heard an agreement on the part of the Indians to accept his proclamation.

174. Believing that he had achieved a bloodless coup, what did De Vargas do then?

With this he departed with all his men to seek a similar agreement from other tribes around the area and to gather the settlers down in El Paso who were bound for Santa Fe. Seventy families, many headed by widows, were prepared to return to Santa Fe, a total of about eight hundred people. In October 1693, after eight months of delay, they departed from El Paso.

175. In what way were the good intentions of de Vargas thwarted?

When de Vargas returned to Santa Fe, it was the dead of winter and he set up tents around the plaza and approached the Indians again, reminding them of their agreement to accept the conditions he had outlined. The Indians refused to leave the Palace of the Governors. After two weeks of negotiations to no avail and facing his own problems with small children dying of exposure in the tents, de Vargas, though initially full of good intentions, finally resorted to a tried and true method of imposing his will. On the morning of December 29, 1693, he initiated a fierce battle.

176. What events brought about the end of the Pueblo self-rule?

The Pueblo Indians were not unified as they had been in 1680, to their disadvantage. The battle waged on all that day. In the morning, the Spaniards scaled the walls. Seeing no hope of victory, the Indian governor named "Jose" hanged himself. By afternoon, the battle was over. What de Vargas had not been able to take by negotiation; he took by force and punished the Indians who had opposed him—about seventy men. The rest of the region was secured in rapid order.

177. Why is this reconquest of New Mexico still referred to as a bloodless one?

Before de Vargas had taken the city by force, back in the fall when he was still content with his peaceful reconquest, de Vargas had written a dispatch to Mexico City announcing his bloodless triumph.

178. Why is a holiday dedicated to the Virgin of the Rosary?

It is believed that the Virgin of the Rosary, commonly known as "La Conquistadora" helped de Vargas in his victory over the Indians. Even today, a holiday is celebrated in her honor.

179. What surprising development occurred almost immediately after the reconquest of New Mexico?

De Vargas who had wanted so badly to go to New Mexico wanted as desperately to move on to more prestigious assignments and petitioned as much from the king. He suggested that Manila in the Philippines might be to his liking or even Guatemala.

180. What happened to this request for a change of assignment?

While his request was making its way through the bureaucracy of Mexico City and Spain, de Vargas changed his mind and wanted to stay in New Mexico. Unhappily for him, it was his first request that was acted on and a new governor was designated for New Mexico.

181. Who was the new governor-designate and how did he behave toward de Vargas?

Pedro Rodriguez Cubero had long coveted the post of governor. He, at last, had his wishes fulfilled. With the aim to discredit the former governor, Cubero spread enough ill will and calumny around to get de Vargas imprisoned in one of the towers of the Palace. Many charges were leveled against de Vargas: misuse of royal funds, abuse of authority, favoritism and instigating sedition among colonists and Indians.

182. How was Cubero able to keep the former governor in prison without the outside world knowing about it?

Diego de Vargas was kept in a small cell in solitary confinement. No one in Mexico City or Spain knew of this imprisonment and Cubero prohibited all communication with and about de Vargas. While de Vargas was in captivity in Santa Fe, he was being honored in Spain. In 1698, the king granted him a noble title.

183. When and how did de Vargas finally get released from prison?

At last in 1700, de Vargas was released from prison. He then traveled to Mexico City to live quietly with friends. Two years later, he was finally exonerated of all accusations against him. In 1704, after his death, an inventory was made of his possessions. It was revealed that he owned forty-one books—an astonishingly large number by the standards of the day. Another governor in the 19th Century—Lew Wallace—would also prove to be a man of letters. Curiously, both would be eager to leave Santa Fe.

184. How did the reconquest affect the population of New Mexico?

With the reconquest, more Spaniards came to New Mexico seeking land. A land-grant system was devised to accommodate the new arrivals. The Pueblo Indians and the Spaniards lived in relative peace in the following years. Attacks, however, from the Apache and the Navajo and increasingly from the Comanche continued.

185. What events were responsible for drawing the attention of Spain away from New Mexico?

In the ensuing years—the late 1600s, Spain became less concerned with New Mexico as its attention was drawn to the growing threats of the French and Indians in Texas. Just as Spain expanded into Texas in response to a foreign threat, so it acquired western Louisiana for purely defensive reasons.

186. Who was Pedro de Villasur?

With rumors that the French were operating among the Pawnee Indians in the central plains, a young lieutenant from Santa Fe named Don Pedro de Villasur took a small army and started to explore the area northeast of the Platte River in present-day Nebraska. The Pawnees fell upon the expedition and killed more than thirty soldiers among them was Villasur.

187. What were the consequences of this massacre?

Governor Valverde was criticized for having sent such an inexperienced young lieutenant on such a hazardous mission. A fine was imposed on the governor of fifty pesos to pay for charity masses for the souls of the dead soldiers.

188. How did this event change the attitude of the French and the Spanish?

This event made the French see the vulnerability of the Spanish on one hand and the possibility of extending their trade, which they hoped, would bring, in payment for their goods, with silver from the mines of Chihuahua. The Spanish, on their side, became more resolved to strengthen their defenses and not allow any contact at all with the French. The borders would remain sealed to foreigners.

189. What changes marked the 18th Century for the inhabitants of New Mexico?

The 18th Century was a time for growth and development for New Mexico. There was considerable trading on the Camino Real. The settlers awaited the arrival of the supply caravan from Mexico with great anticipation. It arrived, as records show, approximately every three years.

190. Was this century also marked by population growth?

The population in Santa Fe doubled to 2,542 residents during the century.

191. What language changes were noted among the settlers?

It was noted that among the changes that had taken place among the settlers, there was the change in language. The linguistic phenomenon was that with little contact with the outside Spanish-speaking world, the Spanish language in New Mexico had become more countrified. Vocabulary became simplified; Indian words were adopted. The overall effect was that the manner of speaking became less gracious and less courtly.

192. What useful lessons did the Spaniards learn from the Indians?

The land and its natives had a powerful impact on the Spaniards. For example, the Spaniards came from a land that was very arid in parts but never did they find the need to deal with desert conditions like those in New

Mexico. From the natives, they learned the judicious use of that precious commodity—water.

193. What did the lack of water teach the Spaniards about cooperation?

In the high mountain villages of New Mexico, the paucity of farmland and the need to share water put a premium on cooperation and intensified communitarian traditions, including communal ownership of land.

194. How did the mutual need for security foster cooperation?

In protecting themselves from the raiding Apache, the Spaniards had a common bond with the Pueblo Indians. Unlike the English settlers of the Northeast who had little sustained contact with the local Indian tribes, Spaniards remained in close contact with the Pueblo Indians.

195. What more did the Spanish homemakers learn from the Indians?

Spanish women learned to plaster their adobe houses from the Indians. The Spaniards learned how to use locally-procured drugs which were previously unknown to them.

196. How did the reign of Philip III differ from that of his father, Philip II, in matters of expansion?

The greatness of the Spanish Empire under Philip II became less extended under his son Philip III. Sustaining such an enormous presence in the Americas was costly. The Church was eager to spend the king's riches as long as it was building churches and saving souls. The empire had grown too big and unmanageable. Spain had trouble at home and wars were draining the royal treasury.

197. What was Bernardo de Galvez's new policy?

In 1786, Bernardo de Galvez, the Viceroy of New Spain, devised a new policy for dealing with the warring Indians in New Mexico. He had learned from the French and English on the Apache frontier in Louisiana several years before. His policy was to use trade rather than war to maintain harmonious relations with the natives. It was important to make the Indians dependent on the Spaniards for satisfying their needs. This included selling the Indians guns and gunpowder and making them reliant on Spaniards as well for procuring these new arms.

198. What were the policies of Governor Anza in regard to relationships with the Indians?

Under Juan Bautista Anza, Governor of New Mexico from 1778 to 1787, a policy of conciliation and negotiation replaced force as the cornerstone of this new association with the Indians. It was Governor Anza who had forged a lasting peace with the western Comanche who had been threatening the province for so many years. Anza could not blame the settlers from spreading themselves out along the fertile banks of the Rio Grande but he felt that he could not give adequate protection to these people. Every time the Indians raided the farms, the settlers would demand protection from the army.

199. What were Governor Anza's plans for urban change?

Anza had long believed that urban renewal was needed to provide the citizens of New Mexico with security. He developed a plan for moving all the settlers up from their homes along the Rio Grande and housing them on the high ground south of the Santa Fe River. When the citizens heard of this plan, they complained loudly to Mexico City and the development never took place.

200. Why was Governor Fernando de la Concha accused of heresy?

Although the Inquisition had put into effect a ban on any foreigner entering the province without permission, Governor Fernando de la Concha defied the ban by having dealings with Frenchmen from New Orleans. He was accused of being a heretic because in front of witnesses he once said, "The masses said by New Mexico friars were worth about as much as what my horse might say."

10

Education

---

201. How might we evaluate the education of the early settlers in Santa Fe?

By our standards today, we might consider the educated man of the early sixteen hundreds to be poorly prepared for roles of leadership. The question of educating the poor never arose and since there was no middle class, the wealthy cornered the market. In matters of hygiene, for example, the poor were again disadvantaged—although the upper class was not that far ahead.

202. Who was educated or thought worthy of education?

Well into the last century, formal education was reserved for the wealthy. This is still true in many parts of the world today. Of that small population, only the male members of the family were considered worthy of schooling. It may be argued that informal education takes place all the time, but the schooling of a gentleman was more formally provided.

203. What part did the Church play in education?

Most often it was the Church that taught the tenets of religion, language, including Latin and Greek and philosophy, when this did not contradict the teachings of the Church.

204. How were the poor educated during the early settlements of the Southwest?

The poor had their church and the civil authority as well, both of which demanded obedience. From the earliest age, the poor were taught to respect their betters and it was not difficult to understand that a man on horseback was to be held in awe. The very name of "gentleman" in Spanish denotes a man on horseback—"caballero." The slightest disrespect or perceived disrespect toward a caballero would earn the transgressor the flat side of a sword across his back.

205. How did the attitude of the Spanish invaders affect their ability to dominate?

At the time when Spain was expanding its reach across the seas, it was the attitude of the invaders that helped impose their will. They demanded only what they believed was their due. Much of what we consider today to be cruel and needlessly overbearing behavior was not considered so at the time. The native populations of New Mexico had no such frame of reference. They were not raised in a two-tier system of the haves and the have-nots.

206. What might have been the reaction of the Indians when faced with this attitude of superiority?

"Why would these strangers take our food?" The natives might ask. "Let them grow their own." So it was not through reasoning that they would understand but rather through force. The native populations understood force, for hadn't they themselves imposed their might on weaker tribes and taken what they wanted from them?

207. Did the Spaniards extend their education to the Indian tribes?

We can only speculate as to what kind of world the Spanish would have created in New Mexico had they led by educating the Indians and provided positive examples for them rather than those of brute force.

208. What stood in the way of bringing education to the Indians?

The Spaniards did not seem committed for the long haul. The civil and religious leaders had pressing agendas of their own. The civil authorities were being judged by the amount of riches they could bring into the coffers of the Crown. The religious leaders were counting the souls they had saved from the fires of hell.

209. Was there no kindness or goodness shown by either side?

The first reactions were those of surprise and apprehension. On both sides there were glimmers of the goodness that was innate in their natures had they not allowed other imperatives to interfere. The natives were curious and generous with the first foreigners they saw, bringing them food and drink. The settlers taught the natives about other plants that would do well in the dry soil other than their native maize and squash.

11

Mining

210. When did New Mexico begin its mining exploration?

Although Coronado did not find streets glistening with gold as he had hoped and Oñate could not coax silver from the earth, mines did exist in New Mexico as early as 1685. The first mining activity of lasting importance began in 1804 in the copper deposits of Santa Rita, in the southwestern part of the state.

211. When was gold discovered in New Mexico?

In 1828, gold was discovered in the Ortiz Mountains between Albuquerque and Santa Fe. This remains today the oldest gold-mining area in the United States. On October 19th, 1903, the newspaper headlines read: "Bonanza near Capital City. Gold and Silver Vein Seven Feet Wide and Six Thousand Feet Long Struck Four Miles Northeast of the Plaza. Gold Runs Ninety-Nine Percent to One of Silver." By the time, New Mexico became a territory of the United States, its annual gold production was valued at three million dollars.

212. How did the work get done in the mines?

From the beginning of mining in the state, Indians worked the mines and foreigners were prohibited from mining activity. There is a story of an Indian who fell sick and was taken to Fort Union for medical care. He later returned with a pretty rock to give as payment for his care. The rock contained gold and a rush soon began to the area.

213. How extensive was the discovery of gold in New Mexico?

After 1828, discovery after discovery took place and soon twenty-three of the present-day state's thirty-two counties were mining gold. The areas northeast of Taos, northeast of Santa Fe and in the southwestern corner of the state had the most important concentrations. The Spanish conquistadors were not wrong about gold; unfortunately, they arrived too early on the scene.

214. When was silver discovered in the state?

Silver, so eagerly sought by Oñate throughout the New Mexico Province and as far west as California, was not found until 1863 in Magdalena and Socorro. Silver City was to become the center of the silver mining activity. Grant County became the center of copper mining and much later, lead and zinc were mined.

215. What role did coal play in supplying energy to New Mexico?

There is no way of knowing how long the residents of New Mexico used coal for heating. We know that during the Civil War coal was used in the army camps for fuel. In Colfax County near Raton the first real coal mining took place. The arrival of the railroads between 1879 and 1882 put coal mining on a solid footing.

12

Further Expansion

216. How did the Burr Conspiracy benefit its plotters?

In 1806, a good deal of attention was being given to the holdings of Spain in the Southwest. One aspect of the infamous Burr Conspiracy, the alleged effort by Aaron Burr to capture Spanish possessions in the Southwest was to bring riches to the plotters by despoiling the Spanish empire in America.

217. What great expansion took place at the beginning of the 19th Century?

It was the Louisiana Purchase in 1803. Thomas Jefferson had stretched the United States Constitution around the sprawling Louisiana territory, which was still poorly defined. This was the disputed territory that the French had ceded to Spain in 1762 rather than let it fall into the hands of the British.

218. Who was Zebulon Pike?

Zebulon Pike was a young U.S. Army lieutenant who enjoyed exploration but was not particularly politically astute. He has been called a "poor man's Lewis and Clark." Pike, son of a veteran of the American Revolution, had orders to investigate the sources of the Arkansas and Red Rivers.

219. What was Pike's mission?

With twenty-three men, he crossed the plains to the foot of the Rockies. Most Americans know only that a mountain peak in Colorado is named after him. Whether he was a knowing foil in the hands of his superior, General Wilkinson, or not isn't fully known. The General sent Zebulon Pike on an extended information-gathering mission into the Spanish-controlled Southwest. Pike and his companion, Dr. John Hamilton Robinson had concocted a false reason of wanting to collect a debt in Santa Fe.

220. What happened to Pike when he crossed into Spanish territory and began to build a fort?

Spain jealously guarded its borders to Texas and New Mexico from outsiders. The Commander of the Internal Provinces of New Spain, Nemesio Salcedo had Pike and party arrested and interred in the Palace of the Governors, despite Pike's claim that they had lost their way.

221. When did the American exploration begin in earnest?

Between 1807 and 1821, due to the exploration of Zebulon Pike, several Americans attempted trade in New Mexico and to trap in the streams.

222. Who were these explorers?

They were mountain men or trappers and were the precursors of the heavy influx of American immigration. These men were of many different races and cultural backgrounds. They knew no borders or boundaries but moved freely as they pleased. It was not just to New Mexico that they traveled but also throughout the Southwest.

223. What did these mountain men do?

They led a rough and dangerous life and oral history abounds with their pursuits. They trapped beaver for the pelts and all but depleted the supply. Trapping and trading, they gradually and steadily pushed the limits of an outside civilization westward well into Spanish territory.

224. What happened to change the destiny of the United States?

In the first two decades of the 19th Century Spain's New World Empire crumbled. In 1821, New Spain (Mexico) declared its independence from Spain, following the other former Spanish colonies.

225. What lands did Mexico then take over?

Most of what is now the American West, including all of Nevada, Utah and parts of Colorado, Kansas and Wyoming, as well as the four border states of California, Arizona, New Mexico and Texas, went under the jurisdiction of independent Mexico.

226. How did the Mexicans celebrate their independence from Spain?

Thomas James described the celebration of Mexico's independence from Spain. He tells how it was his idea to erect a seventy-foot liberty pole and run up the first flag: "No Italian carnival ever exceeded this celebration in thoughtlessness, vice and licentiousness of every description." Governor Melgares called it an unforgettable day. There were salvos, processions and pageants and Indian dances in the plaza.

227. How did Mexico deal with persistent rumors of Spain's desire to retake its lands?

In late 1827, there were rumors that Spain planned to invade and reconquer Mexico. In preparation of this eventuality, the Mexican National Congress decreed the expulsion of peninsular Spaniards from the republic. Several Spanish Franciscans left New Mexico as a result.

228. What did Texas do to extend its land?

Texas, seeing the opportunity to avenge the loss of lives at the Alamo and seek independence for itself rebelled successfully against Mexico in 1836. Ten years later, in 1846, American troops invaded New Mexico, southern Arizona and California.

229. What were Spain's difficulties at this time?

Mexico seized the opportunity for declaring its independence from Spain. The French Revolution and Napoleonic Wars diverted Spain's attention from its colonies. Ferdinand VII was removed from the Spanish throne and was replaced by Joseph Bonaparte, Napoleon's brother.

230. Who was Miguel Hidalgo y Costilla?

His name stands out among many important figures of this period. He was called the leader of the movement for Mexican Independence. He was a liberal priest from the Parish of Delores. It was Father Hidalgo who distributed the Grito de Delores—a call for social and economic reform.

231. How did Father Hidalgo gain support for his cause?

In an attempt to gain more supporters for his cause he said: "My friends and countrymen: Neither the king nor tributes exist for us any longer. We have borne this shameful tax, which only suits slaves, for three centuries as a sign of tyranny and servitude; a terrible stain, which we shall know how to wash away...."

232. How was Father Hidalgo made to pay for his actions?

Before he was executed in 1811, Father Hidalgo was made to recant by the Inquisitors. In a statement he said: "I am repentant for the incalculable ills which have originated out of the frenzy which possessed me to break so scandalously with the King, the nation and Christian morality."

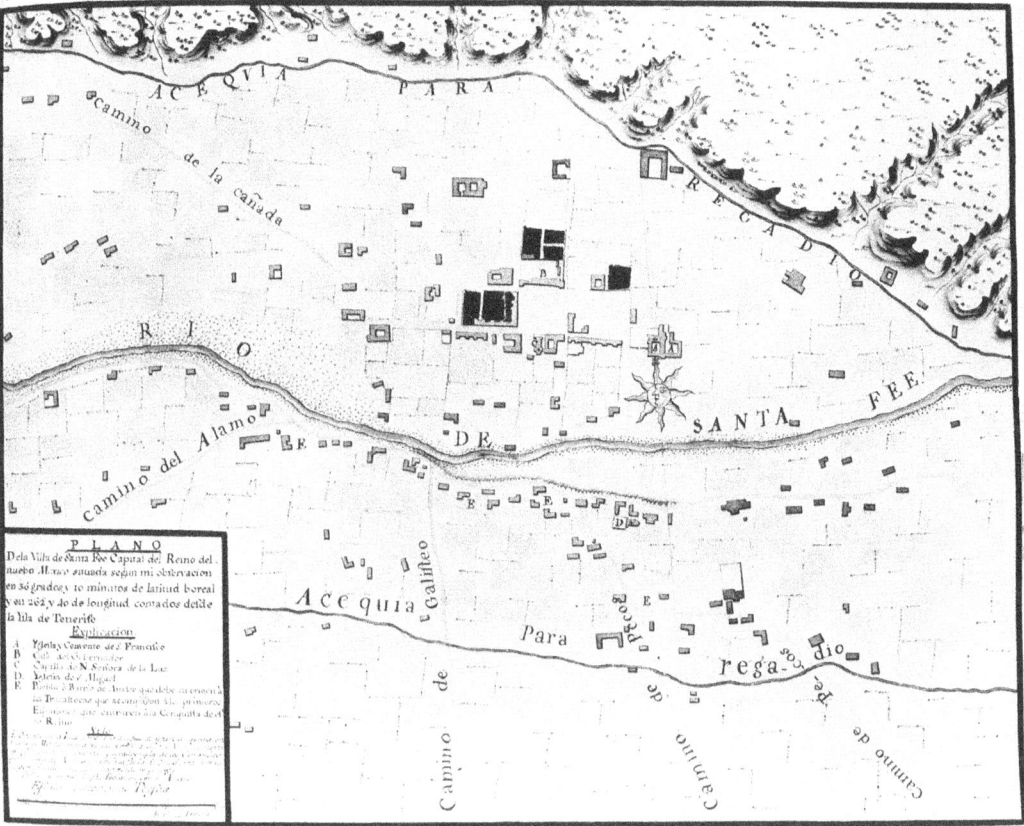

1766 map of Santa Fe drawn by Joseph de Urrútia.

Map of Santa Fe in August, 1846. From *Doniphan's Expedition* by John T. Hughes, 1850.

SANTA FE.

An early impression of Santa Fe. From *Report of Lieut. J. W. Abert of His Examination of New Mexico in the Years 1846–1847.*

GENERAL VIEW OF SANTA FE.

General view of Santa Fe. From *Harper's Weekly*, September, 1870.

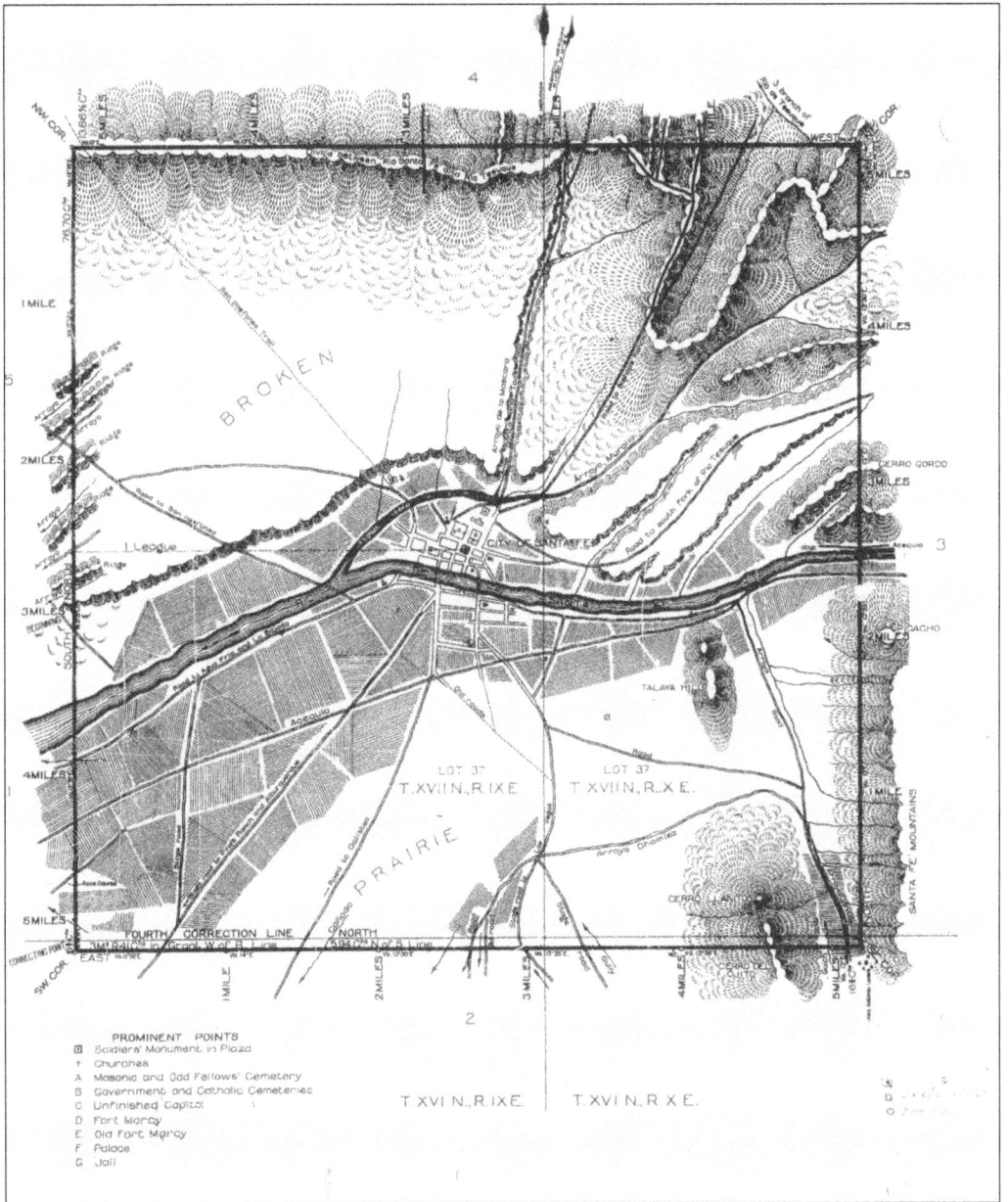

Plat of the Santa Fe grant. Bureau of Land Management, Santa Fe.

Ft. Marcy.   Episcopal Church.   Cañon of the Rio Santa Fe.
St. Vincent's Hospital.   Cathedral San Francisco (See of S
Palace Hotel.   Academy and Convent Sis
Masonic and Old Fellows' Cemetery.   Spanish Government Palace.   Plaza and Center of
Gas Works.   State House Grounds.   U. S. Military Reservation, H'd Qrs. Dist. N
Tri-Centenary Celetbraion Grounds, 1883.   Presbyterian Church.   Texas, Santa Fe

CITY OF SANTA

(COPYRIG

Impression of Santa Fe in 1882. From *Illustrated New Mexico, 1885* by W. G. Ritch.

San Miguel Cemetery.   El Atalaya.
ta Fe.) Bishop's Garden.   Camping Ground U. S. Army, Aug. 18, 1846.   Santa Fe Trail.
s Loretto. San Miguel Church and College.   Rio de Santa Fe.
iness.   Territorial Peniten iary.
                                                  Congregational Church.
d Northern R. R.   Guadalupe Church. A. T. and S. F. R. R. Depot.
         Methodist Church.   U. S. Indian School. (Gov. Vigil Place.

E, NEW MEXICO.
D.)   *Presented by the Bureau of Immigration, New Mexico.*

A map of Santa Fe, ca 1910s. Courtesy of Robert L Spude.

13

The Santa Fe Trail

233. What was Spain's policy on trade?

During the years of Spanish control of New Mexico, the Spanish regime was very restrictive about trade. New Mexico could only trade with Mexico, which was designed to keep the proceeds within the provinces of New Spain. All overtures from the United States or France were discouraged. The towns south of Santa Fe on the Camino Real such as El Paso and Chihuahua began to thrive with trade.

234. What changed after 1821?

When Mexico declared its independence from Spain in 1821, it took possession of New Mexico as well. That same year trade was encouraged and began to grow with the United States. Governor Facundo Melgares foresaw the great possibilities of opening the pathway to the northeast, although the prairie was not without danger and risk.

235. Who was William Becknell?

In 1821, William Becknell, of Franklin, Missouri advertised for men to accompany him to the southern Rockies for the purpose of trading horses and mules and catching wild animals. Unknown to Becknell was the fact that the lands he wished to visit were no longer in the hands of the Spanish and the very restrictive trade laws they enforced. At a place near Raton Pass, Becknell and his men were stopped by Mexican soldiers, who escorted the startled men into Santa Fe.

236. How successful was Becknell's first trading attempt in the Southwest?

The city was in full celebration of the independence of Mexico from Spain. Instead of selling horses, Becknell sold everything else he had in his wagons including calico and various sundry items that had been unavailable prior to this time in Santa Fe. Seeing an excellent possibility for business, Becknell returned again to Santa Fe, this time with three freight wagons and a pack train loaded with $5,000 worth of merchandise and again turned a handsome profit. William Becknell is today known as the "Father of the Santa Fe Trail" for his pioneering spirit and sound business sense. With his success, many wagons began to travel the long journey from Missouri to Santa Fe.

237. What were the concerns and dangers of the southern route of the Santa Fe Trail?

The concerns were many. The shorter of the two trails was the southern route, which led through the Cimarron Desert. The advantage was that the wagons could negotiate the desert paths more easily but the drawbacks were a lack of water and the danger of Indian raids.

238. How much better was the northern route?

The northern route through the Colorado passes was free of Indian raids and there was plenty of water but the mountain passes were so difficult that at times, the wagons had to be lowered over the cliffs by rope.

239. Who was Augustus Storrs?

Augustus Storrs who later became the first U.S. Consul for Santa Fe turned an investment of $35,000 into $180,000 by trading on the trail.

240. How is Josiah Gregg remembered in the history of Santa Fe?

He was an important person of trade and commerce of this period. His writings have contributed greatly to the understanding and appreciation of the Southwest. His book *Commerce of the Prairies* is a classic. It was Gregg who brought the first printing press to the territory.

241. How did the Indian tribes react to the many wagons traveling on the trail?

Trade on the Santa Fe Trail became so important to the economy of the region that an attempt was made to pay the Indians for the right of passage through their lands. The Kiowa and Comanche had been raiding and killing many of the traders. The Indians took the money but paid no attention to the agreement.

242. When did the traders request assistance from the military?

It was not until 1828 that military escorts began to accompany the wagons to assure their safe arrival. The traders on the trail would elect a captain of the caravan whose powers were undefined and vague but who had the responsibility of directing the travel, selecting the camping sites and making general decisions on a daily basis. All members of the caravan were required to stand guard duty. When the party had crossed the dangerous plains, the organization was dissolved.

243. How did trade in Santa Fe affect other markets?

As a byproduct of the heavy trade with Santa Fe, other markets, further south also benefited from the goods coming from the north, as long as peace existed between the Anglos of Missouri and the Mexicans. Santa Fe became the nucleus of trade, rather than the end of the line.

244. What dollar amount was traded on the Santa Fe Trail?

At the height of the trade on the Santa Fe Trail in 1846, a total of 628 wagons carried just under a million dollars worth of goods. The wagons would often assume a military formation, sometimes ten or more wagons abreast as they crossed the wide plains. There was security in numbers.

245. How did Marion Sloan Russell describe her first glimpse of Santa Fe?

As a child of seven, Marion Sloan Russell arrived in Santa Fe in 1852 by wagon. She later described her first impressions: "How our hearts waited for a sight of Santa Fe of our dreams. We thought it would be a city and waited breathlessly for the first sight of towers and tall turrets. We crossed a water ditch...then passed a great wooden gateway that arched high above us. We were in Santa Fe."

246. How did Susan Magoffin describe the Apache raids?

Danger was ever-present on the trail. In her diary, Susan Shelby Magoffin told how her brother James had been robbed of everything he owned by the Apache Indians but was lucky to have his life spared. This was unusual because the scalp was considered the finest trophy.

247. What did James White write about his dangerous experience on the trail?

The story about James White who was a merchant of Independence, Missouri and Santa Fe is a troubling one. In October 1849, while traveling with his wife and young daughter, Apache Indians—at a place where the caravan was supposed to be out of danger—attacked them. All eight men in the caravan were killed and the woman and child were taken captive. When the murders were reported, Kit Carson and some other guides tried to rescue the woman and her child but as they were speaking with the Indians, the woman began to run toward her rescuers but was immediately killed by the Apache. The child was never found.

248. Did European settlers make their way to the Southwest?

Settlers from Europe, especially from Germany were among the founding families of the city's mercantile businesses. Excellent books have been written about the German-Jewish pioneers and how they worked hard and gave generously to the growth of the city, whether it was in support of Archbishop Lamy's construction of St. Francis Cathedral or the pledge to bring the railroad to Santa Fe.

249. Had the path of the Santa Fe Trail been used prior to the 1800s?

The Santa Fe Trail was the only easy route between the Rowe bluffs and the Sangre de Cristo Mountains for those making their way to Pueblo Indian country. This passage had been used for thousands of years as a main trade route between the Great Plains and the Rio Grande. Later the Atchison, Topeka and Santa Fe Railway followed this route.

14

Unrest, Rebellion and War

250. Why was Governor Perez unpopular with the people of Santa Fe?

In 1835, Colonel Albino Perez was sent by officials in Mexico to take charge of the departmental affairs of New Mexico. Governor Perez was a man of high ideals and had some good plans for public education. Santa Feans disliked him. He was not a native and the changes he brought were unpopular. To make matters worse, the new governor had to impose new tax laws.

251. What did the Santa Feans do about this unpopular governor?

Governor Perez's changes brought about a revolt. It began in the Chimayo-Santa Cruz de la Canada area north of Santa Fe. Perez was unable to put down the uprising. He fled the capital, was caught and assassinated near Agua Fria. What had started out as a plan to support public education in New Mexico by direct taxation progressed to mandates for punishment of nonperformance of military education and then ended with the killing of the messenger. It was a brutal death—decapitation with Perez's head carried around on a pike.

252. Did the Santa Feans do without a governor?

No. Manuel Armijo who had been governor of New Mexico was called upon to bring peace and order to New Mexico after the revolt. He was to punish the leaders and assume the functions of governor once again. The rebels had installed Jose Gonzalez to take the place of Perez. When Armijo took charge, Gonzalez was put to death, as were other leaders.

253. How did the governor deal with the Texas land-grab of 1841?

In 1841, a Texan incursion tested Armijo's resolve. The governor, however, was able to push back the Texans with little difficulty. However, the writing was now on the wall. The Americans were coming. Fully armed with a belief that Manifest Destiny was to be fulfilled—stretching American soil from sea to sea—the United States was in a frenzy of land grabbing. Mexico, claiming that the United States had been a bad and greedy neighbor broke off diplomatic relations with the United States in March 1845.

254. When did the United States declare war on Mexico?

In May 1846, Congress, at the urging of President Polk, declared war on Mexico. A month later, the Army of the West set out for New Mexico over the Santa Fe Trail. Leading the army was Brigadier-General Stephen Watts Kearny from Leavenworth, Missouri.

255. What was General Kearny's background?

Stephen Watts Kearny was born August 30, 1794 in Newark, New Jersey but lived in the West during most of his years of service. He was a soldier, explorer, builder, writer and statesman. He commanded the Army of the West and was called the "Father of the U.S. Cavalry."

256. What was the composition of Kearny's army?

After ten years in the West, Kearny had already become legendary, and his skill and fame as a leader was so extensive that men fought to fill the ranks of his army. Kearny had about 300 army regulars, most of them experienced in western duty and some inexperienced frontiersmen.

257. What did Kearny do when he heard the size of the Mexican army?

Kearny had heard that a Mexican army of about 3,000 was marching north from Chihuahua. Kearny had no way of verifying this news but he did not want to waste any time. Leaving Fort Leavenworth, he kept his troops moving until they reached Bent's Fort in present-day Colorado. He had covered more than 550 miles.

258. How did Kearny manage to get the governor to leave Santa Fe peacefully?

Rumors still persist, although no proof exists, that Armijo was given a case of gold in exchange for not opposing the will of General Kearny. The following day, Armijo departed down the Camino Real with a bodyguard of soldiers instead of fighting for Santa Fe at the Apache Pass.

259. Was there any written correspondence prior to this time between Kearny and Armijo?

On August1, 1846, Kearny wrote to Governor Armijo from Bent's Fort. He wrote: "By annexation of Texas to the United States, the Rio Grande from its mouth to its source forms...the boundary between her and Mexico, and I come by orders...to take possession of the country, over part of which you are now presiding as Governor...." The letter held the proverbial carrot in one hand saying that all consideration would be made in the transfer of control in a "benevolent" manner, and a whip in the other hand threatening reprisals and punishment should the United States forces encounter opposition.

260. What was the legacy of General Kearny?

General Kearny died on October 31, 1848. Kearny's military expeditions served to enlarge the territorial holdings of the United States by more than a million square miles.

261. Where was Fort Marcy built?

Fort Marcy, named for Secretary of War, William L. Marcy, was hurriedly built on the high ground north of the Plaza. It was never garrisoned and never used to defend Santa Fe. It seems that the troops stationed at Fort Marcy were a constant concern to the citizens of the capital. Most of the troops were transferred to Fort Union in 1851.

262. How did Lieutenant Colonel Sumner describe Fort Marcy?

When Lieutenant Colonel Sumner took up his new assignment as commander of the Military Department of New Mexico, he showed his dismay in writing: "I reached Santa Fe, on the 19th of July and assumed post at Santa Fe, that sink of vice and extravagance, and to remove the troops and public property to this place (Fort Union)."

263. When did Fort Marcy close?

Fort Marcy was closed in 1867. With whatever ease General Kearny had in taking Santa Fe, all was not well. A number of the descendents of the Spanish settlers were upset about giving up Santa Fe to the Anglo-Americans. They felt more closely allied to Mexico. In December 1846, these prominent citizens plotted against the newly arrived Americans to undermine their authority. There are several stories about how the plot was discovered. Suffice it to say that the Americans learned about it and arrested the plotters.

264. How did the Pueblo Indians react to American rule?

More serious was the Pueblo Indian reaction to the new governor of the New Mexico Territory. Incited to riot, these Indians attacked Governor Charles Bent in his Taos home, shot him with arrows and scalped him.

265. How was this event described?

Rosemary Nusbaum describes the holidays that the Bent brothers planned to have at Taos where Charles Bent who had recently been appointed governor of the territory by General Kearny was to meet with his family: "William Bent decided to go to Taos for a few days of rest with his Mexican wife Ignacia and their three children. At the time, Kit Carson's wife Josefa was staying with them. Bent (the new governor) knew there were no troops in Taos. At dawn on January 19th , a howling mob of Mexican and Indian supporters came to the house. He stepped outside and an arrow killed him."

266. What did the Indians hope to achieve with this revolt?

It is uncertain whether this act was directed against the Bents—Charles, William and George or whether it was the way the Taos Indians wanted to show their special welcome for the new American regime. The revolt spread quickly but the army responded without hesitation. In late January 1847, following the battles at Santa Cruz de la Canada and Embudo, the rebels retreated. On February 3rd, the insurrection was broken and many prisoners were taken. The prisoners were tried for treason and murder and many were hanged.

267. How did the character of Santa Fe change during these times?

With the arrival of the American Army and the building of Fort Marcy, many more settlers flowed into Santa Fe. Bars and gambling houses became the gathering places for these new arrivals. The strictly religious nature of the capital as it had flourished under Spanish and Mexican rule was changing. The cultural clash of Anglo-American and Hispanic-American became evident.

268. What status did this new American territory have?

It was in 1850 that Congress recognized the territorial status of New Mexico, although General Kearny had declared it unofficially earlier. It was also the first year that New Mexico petitioned for statehood but was ignored.

269. What was the war with Mexico really about?

In putting the war between the United States and Mexico into the perspective of more than a hundred and fifty years, we see that Americans still call it the "Mexican War" while Mexicans refer to it as the "U.S. Invasion." Even the most casual reader of history cannot help but conclude that the United States was bent on fighting Mexico for land.

270. What gave the United States an excuse for going to war?

On April 25, 1846, the opportunity presented itself. Mexico had given the U.S. the excuse it needed. Mexican soldiers under the command of General Mariano Arista crossed the Rio Grande and attacked an American patrol, killing or wounding sixteen men. This was the opportunity President Polk was waiting for. In his war message to Congress on May 11th, he said: "Mexico... has invaded our territory and shed American blood upon American soil."

271. What was the result of this war?

Very quickly American armies invaded Mexico, crossing its northern frontier and eventually moving inland from its eastern coast. When General Winfield Scott marched his army from Veracruz to Mexico City, the war was over. In a treaty, the U.S. paid Mexico $15,000,000 and for that sum received the vast northern provinces of California and New Mexico. The Rio Grande was recognized as the international border between the two countries.

272. How did the Pueblo Indians adjust to the Americans?

Under the new American regime, the nomad tribes were being defeated and confined to reservations. The Pueblo people were finding it difficult to adjust to American rule. Whatever privilege they may have enjoyed under the Mexican regime was not at all guaranteed under the Americans. Of major concern was the protection of rights and property of the Pueblo Indians.

273. Why were the Americans so seemingly indifferent?

There was so little understanding of the Native Americans in Washington and little willingness to see the difference between the peaceful Pueblo people and the war-like nomads. These concerns were some of the first to be addressed by New Mexico's first Indian agent, James S. Calhoun.

274. How was this understanding gap bridged?

With the Treaty of Guadalupe Hidalgo, protection was also assured to those persons who became citizens of the United States. However, respecting the land grant arrangements made by the Spaniards or Mexicans proved to be more complicated than the Americans originally thought. First of all, there was a clear difference between the systems of law pertaining to property.

275. What was the Gadsden Purchase Treaty?

The Gadsden Purchase Treaty, signed in 1854, was named after James

Gadsden who was appointed by the President of the United States to draw up an agreement between the U.S. and Mexico. The purpose of the treaty was to outline in careful detail the acquiring of a new section of land, which the United States wished to purchase from Mexico. The Treaty contained nine articles outlining the exact location of the land, points that required clarification between the Treaty of Guadalupe Hidalgo and the Gadsden Purchase. Article three described the money to be paid to Mexico.

276. How much money was involved?

Of the ten million dollars, which was to be paid in New York, seven million would be paid upon signing the treaty and the remaining three million dollars as soon as the boundary line was surveyed, marked and legally established. Care was given to make certain that individuals, companies and all concerned would not be negatively affected when traveling along the Colorado River, navigating the Gulf of California or by land travel but at all times respecting the governments of both countries.

277. What was the status of agriculture in the territory of New Mexico?

In 1850, the official number of farms in the territory was 3,750. Ten years later that number had almost doubled. Although the Civil War interrupted the growth of farms and the transportation of produce to the markets, the war did help New Mexico increase its cattle raising economy.

278. What was the new requirement for meat?

Soldiers and miners in New Mexico wanted beef. In addition to the needs of soldiers and miners, the government had to feed some 8,500 Indians at Bosque Redondo who were penned up there on a reservation. As it turned out, two Texans—Charles Goodnight and Oliver Loving were the first to reach the cattle markets with their combined herds and drive them into New Mexico.

279. How did the New Mexicans view Texans coming into their territory?

In some respects this influx of Texans and their herds was just another phase in the Anglo invasion of the territory. Within a short time, cattle trails crisscrossed the territory in all directions. One of the most famous of New Mexico's early cattle ranchers was John S. Chisum. His cattle range extended 150 miles, from the Texas border to Fort Sumner and he raised about 60,000 head of cattle a year on this land.

280. What meat economy existed before the arrival of cattle?

Prior to the arrival of the cattlemen, sheep herding dominated the agricultural economy. As early as 1598, Oñate saw that sheep were fully adapted to the semi-arid climate of New Mexico because it was so similar to that of Spain. Some families owned as many as 250,000 head of sheep and enjoyed the large tracts of land they had received as grants from the authorities. Josiah Gregg wrote that there were as many as 500,000 head of sheep exported in one year. With the 1849 gold rush in California another important market for New Mexico mutton was established.

15

Religion and Education in the 19th Century

281. What was the status of religion and education in the mid 1800s?

Cultural heritage extends itself and is transmitted from one generation to the next. In primitive societies, the family and tribe or clan manages to do this. Learning takes place by imitation and practice. In more complex societies, formal institutions are entrusted with much of the socialization process. In the 1850s, New Mexico had no public schools so it was the Church that took the responsibility of teaching the young. The Church has always believed that education is incomplete without the knowledge of religion.

282. What difficulties did the Church encounter during this period in the Southwest?

Unfortunately in virtually every country of the world and during every era, the Church has not been without blemish. During the time of expansion of New Mexico, the Church could not keep up with the needs of the faithful.

283. Under what jurisdiction did the Church in Santa Fe find itself?

While still under Mexican control, Santa Fe came under the direction and the responsibility of the Bishop of Durango in Mexico. Supervision and guidance were impossible at that great distance.

284. How did this lack of supervision affect the clergy?

Many men took vows who had no business doing so. Far from serving as positive examples for the settlers, these persons gave the church a terrible reputation. Well documented are instances where these "priests" violated every tenet of their faith. Many were known to have kept mistresses, were heavy gamblers and addicted to alcohol. With the province of New Mexico becoming a territory of the United States, a number of priests returned to their own country south of the border. Remaining were too few priests, many of whom had strayed from the discipline of the cloth.

285. Who was destined to become an important religious force in New Mexico?

A French-born priest, Jean Baptiste Lamy, was selected by the Vatican to become the Bishop of New Mexico.

286 What was Bishop Lamy's background?

Jean Baptiste's parents were well-to-do peasants from the Massif Central in France. Of their eleven children, only four made it into adulthood. Louis and Baptiste became priests and Marguerite became a nun.

287. Did Lamy travel alone from France?

No. He traveled with his good friend Joseph Priest Machebeuf. After forty-three days crossing the Atlantic, they arrived in New York. It was in this manner that the cleric began his career for the Church. He was to bestride religious life in New Mexico like a colossus.

288. Was Lamy immediately assigned to the Southwest?

No. Eleven years after arriving in America, Jean Baptiste Lamy began his trip to the "Great American Desert" traveling from Cincinnati by riverboat. Pope Pius IX had just recently consecrated him to his bishopric.

289. Did the local church accept him at once?

The rural vicar—Juan Felipe Ortiz announced that Lamy was not the Bishop of Santa Fe and would not be recognized as such. Ortiz told Lamy that Santa Fe still reported to the Bishop of Durango.

290. How did the young bishop react?

Lamy's first battle then was to exercise his authority and claim the diocese of New Mexico, which still included all of present-day Arizona. The land mass was larger than his native France. Bishop Lamy met this challenge with stubbornness, perhaps reflecting the character of the people of Auvergne where he was born.

291. What changes did Bishop Lamy envision for New Mexico?

Bishop Lamy had three main goals for New Mexico. First, he would bring education to Santa Fe. During his first weeks in Santa Fe he realized how important education would be to the people. Education, not just book knowledge, he insisted, but education in Christian amenity. He wrote: "The state of immorality in matters of sex is so deplorable that the most urgent need is too open schools for girls under the direction of Sisters of Charity." He had already been looking for a site to build a convent. As for boys, Lamy wanted a school for them in every parish.

Secondly, Lamy would build a cathedral dedicated to the Patron Saint of Santa Fe—Saint Francis. This cathedral would not be made of adobe but of sandstone, quarried locally. It would have stained glass windows imported from France. La Parroquia, the church, which was to be replaced by the cathedral, had been built in 1710-12 and served as the main house of worship until the arrival of the bishop. Only the chapel, which houses the statue of the Conquistadora, remains today from La Parroquia.

Thirdly, Bishop Lamy would bring order to the religious ranks of Santa Fe. He would reform this holy establishment, which had been allowed to grow stagnant and corrupt. He would remove priests from their posts and unfrock them, some from members of New Mexico's leading families, causing politicians to attempt to oust him. One priest who shocked Bishop Lamy because of an undisciplined lifestyle was Padre Gallegos who lived openly with his mistress. Bishop Lamy excommunicated him.

292. What is the legacy of Archbishop Lamy?

Aside from building a solid clergy, through Lamy's efforts, Santa Fe today has Christus St. Vincent Regional Medical Center, established by the Sisters of Charity; St. Francis Cathedral; Loretto Chapel, built for the Sisters of Loretto and their institution, Loretto Academy for Girls; and St. Michael's College, which is now called the Santa Fe University of Art and Design.

293. Why did the Church take such pains to bring a French bishop to Santa Fe?

It may be of interest to note that the selection of a French-born bishop for Santa Fe may not have been casual. It may very well have been an attempt by the Church to bring some balance to the prevailing Spanish/Mexican influence in the Church. In addition to replacing an adobe church with a Romanesque cathedral, Bishop Lamy modeled the Loretto Chapel on the Sainte Chapelle in Paris.

294. When did St. Vincent's Sanatorium burn down?

It burned down on June 16, 1896. This is how *The New Mexican* reported the incident: "The burning of St. Vincent Sanatorium in this city, on Sunday evening, is not only a serious loss to the noble order of Sisters of Charity, but it is a loss of no slight magnitude to the city of Santa Fe. It is the pioneer institution of the kind in the far west."

295. How important was this institution?

The importance of this institution cannot be overemphasized. Richard Harris writes: "Physicians came to recognize that the high, dry, mild climate was ideal for alleviating the symptoms of lung disease...first the church-owned St. Vincent's Sanatorium and later the renowned Sunmount Sanitarium filled to capacity with refugees from the coal-smoke pollution of the eastern industrial cities, seeking a cure for tuberculosis and other chronic respiratory illnesses."

296. Who built the Loretto Chapel?

It was Projectus Mouly, son of the architect of the cathedral, who undertook the Loretto Chapel. It was a serious responsibility for a youth of eighteen, especially in that his father could not give him guidance. Antoine Mouly was going blind and had to be returned to France. The Chapel is a success in every way. It is today the oldest Gothic structure west of the Mississippi.

297. What is the legend attached to the Loretto Chapel?

There is a legend and like most legends, its telling varies greatly. It seems that the Chapel of Our Lady of Light, called today "The Loretto Chapel" was completed in 1878 but to the dismay of the Sisters, there was no way to access the choir loft. One version tells of a rope ladder that was put into place but it was naturally unacceptable to the Sisters. Since prayer was their way of life, they prayed to St. Joseph, father of Jesus and patron saint of carpenters for a solution to their problem.

298. What was the solution the Sisters found?

On the last day of their novena, a white-bearded man arrived with a few basic tools and asked for work as a carpenter. He was immediately put to work to build a staircase. He worked swiftly and masterfully making a spiral staircase made up of two 360-degree turns leading to the choir loft. Having finished, the man disappeared without being paid for his work. The Sisters believed that it was St. Joseph himself who came to their aid.

299. Was there not a military church in existence at this time?

Yes. There was a church at the site of the present Plaza Galeria at 66 West San Francisco Street. It was called "La Castrense," or "La Capilla de Nuestra Senora de la Luz." This was a Mexican Baroque-style military church, which fronted the plaza from 1760 to 1859. It fell into disrepair and Bishop Lamy ordered it demolished.

300. When did Archbishop Lamy die?

Although Archbishop Lamy lived to a ripe old age and died in February 1888, having traveled thousands of miles to fulfill his mission to New Mexico, he was erroneously reported to have been killed in July of 1867.

301. How was the Archbishop's death reported?

Not many of us are given the opportunity to read our own obituary. Page four of the *New York Herald* on July 19, 1867 reported the following:

"A train was captured last Sunday, near Fort Larned, by the Indians. Bishop Lamy, ten priests and six sisters of charity accompanied the train as passengers en route to Santa Fe. The men were killed, scalped and shockingly mutilated. The females were carried away captives. This information comes through reliable sources."

302. When did the plans for a school for boys materialize?

The original four Christian Brothers came from France to labor under harsh conditions during the first years of the school. The Brothers taught in an adobe hut close to St. Michael's Church in the Analco section of the city. The school received its charter in 1874. It was named after St. Michael's Church.

303. Was the school modeled after French religious schools?

It was founded in the tradition of St. John Baptist de la Salle. About the time the Loretto Chapel was being dedicated, the Christian Brothers began to demolish their old adobe school on College Street and would lay the cornerstone for a two-story building with a third floor incorporated in the mansard.

304. When did St. Michael's School move to its present location?

In 1947 the school, moved from the center of the city to the newly acquired Bruns Army Hospital, which allowed space for its growth. In 1966, the institution changed its name to the College of Santa Fe.

16

Federal Courthouse

305. Under what circumstances was the Federal Courthouse built?

In 1853, as part of a plan to render the architecture of Santa Fe more harmonious with the rest of the United States and thereby make the territory more acceptable for statehood, a building was constructed in the Greek Revival Style to serve as the Territorial Capital.

306. How much money was available for this project?

The project was begun with only twenty thousand dollars. An additional fifty thousand dollars was added for the increased costs.

307. How far did the increased costs go in covering the construction?

Unfortunately, the money could only construct the walls. This structure remained without a roof for thirty years and never served as the territorial capital.

308. When was this building completed?

A temporary roof was added in 1883 but the building was not completed until 1930. It serves quite well today as the federal courthouse.

309. When did Santa Fe celebrate its Tertio-Millennial?

It was in 1883 that Santa Fe celebrated its Tertio-Millennial Celebration. Clearly, the city was in the mood for a big fiesta so the enthusiasts arbitrarily selected the year of 1550 as the beginning of the Spanish occupation of the city. (Actually, it was not until the arrival of Peralta in 1609–1610 that this took place).

310. How did the name Tertio-Millennial come about?

The city planners then calculated that the city was 333 years old or one third of a millennium. That is how they got the name of Tertio-Millennial.

311. What is the Federal Oval?

The construction of the road surrounding the federal courthouse was named the "Federal Oval"—and was used for horse racing and much later for high school track meets. The area became popular for picnics as well.

17

The Buffalo Soldiers

312. How long have black soldiers fought in American armies?

Blacks fought in George Washington's army during the War of
Independence and in every war since then.

313. When was the first regiment of black soldiers organized?

The first black regiment in the United States fought under Colonel
Higginson in 1861 with the South Carolina Volunteers.

314. When were black regiments authorized officially?

Five years later an Act of Congress authorized six regiments of Black
troops—-two of cavalry and four of infantry. It was September 1866 that
the 9th Cavalry Regiment was activated at Greenville, Louisiana.

**315. What factors led these soldiers to perform extraordinary feats in
battle, even under adverse conditions?**

The men carried out their work with older horses and substandard
equipment. Often they were housed in run-down forts. Despite these
drawbacks, they took pride in being entrusted with difficult missions and
accomplished the tasks given to them extremely well and earned the respect
of all those who saw them fight.

316. When did these soldiers fight in New Mexico?
The 9th was transferred to the District of New Mexico during the winter
and spring of 1875–1876 and spent the next six years fighting the Apache.

317. How did these black soldiers get their name?

The Plains Indians began calling the Black cavalrymen "Buffalo Soldiers" and these troops accepted the name and carried it with pride. For the Indians, the buffalo was sacred and the name was a measure of respect.

318. What distinction did the Buffalo Soldiers have in their dedication to duty?

In various archival records throughout Santa Fe, there are many references to the bravery and selflessness of the Buffalo Soldiers. As a point of interest, the 9th and 10th Cavalry had the lowest rate of desertion in the entire army.

18

The Civil War

319. Why did Texas initiate the Civil War in the West?

Texas, living outside the nation it had wished to join thirty years earlier, was ready to spearhead an invasion of New Mexico. Not only did Texas plan to take for itself all the land east of the Rio Grande River but also thought its troops could run through Colorado and cut west to California and seize the gold mines. This was a bold plan but if successful might have added considerable real estate for the Confederacy.

320. When did Texas invade New Mexico?

In July 1861, confederate soldiers from Texas invaded New Mexico Territory. The battle lasted only twelve months.

321. How did the early part of the war progress?

Lieutenant Colonel John R. Baylor led his Confederate forces and succeeded in capturing Albuquerque and Santa Fe. The taking of these two cities was quite an easy operation. A New Orleans newspaper carried the following: "In February, 1861, Colonel John R. Baylor organized the Fourth Regiment of Texas cavalry and with a battalion of six companies marched from San Antonio to El Paso, Texas, capturing forts on the line of march which had been vacated by Union troops...from there the battalion proceeded to New Mexico and captured Fort Fillmore."

322. How did the Texans arm themselves?

Before leaving San Antonio they had raided and seized the U.S. arsenal and barracks.

323. Was New Mexico a match for the Texan Army?

Secretary of War, Simon Cameron, acknowledged that New Mexico was in no condition to resist an attack. The regular troops had been sent out of the territory to fight on other fronts.

324. Why was it pointless for the U.S. Government to send other cavalry troops to New Mexico?

Most of the soldiers were disgruntled, not having received any pay for some time. Because of the long-extended drought in New Mexico, there was little grass for horses to feed on which made sending cavalry regiments senseless.

325. Who was given the command to invade New Mexico?

On July 8th, General H. H. Sibley was given the task by Confederate President Davis who ordered General Sibley to drive the federal forces out of New Mexico. Sibley knew the country well.

326. How did Sibley view this assignment?

It has been speculated that Sibley may have considered the task below him and that he would have preferred to remain in Virginia or go on to Gettysburg for an important campaign.

327. What miscalculation did Sibley make at the outset?

He did not take his task very seriously, partly because he thought the Southwest would be handed to him on a silver platter because of the sympathizers for the Confederate cause. He may not have taken the precautions that Colonel Baylor may have taken.

328. What was the first major battle in New Mexico?

The first major battle of the Civil War in New Mexico was fought at Valverde on February 21, 1862. Commanding the Union forces was Edward R.S. Canby.

329. What did the two commanders have in common?

As often was the case in the Civil War in which brother was sometimes pitted against brother, Henry Sibley and Edward Canby had been close friends, having been to West Point together.

330. What was the result of the battle at Valverde?

The Battle of Valverde was a victory for Sibley's troops during which they destroyed a battery of Union artillery forces. Canby dug in at Fort Craig with more than three thousand men so the Texas soldiers bypassed the fort.

331. What was the Confederate Army's next victory?

The Confederate forces next marched up the Rio Grande. On March 2, 1862, the Confederate flag was raised over Albuquerque after both sides agreed to curtail hostilities and save the city from destruction.

332. What happened at Santa Fe?

Confederate troops lost no time taking Santa Fe and raising their flag—the fourth flag, Spanish, Mexican, Territorial and now Confederate to fly above the Palace of the Governors.

333. Why were the Union forces beaten so quickly?

The Union forces were seriously outnumbered, six hundred Union forces against over a thousand Confederate forces. By most accounts the war in New Mexico should have ended at Santa Fe.

334. What were the Confederate Army's plans after Santa Fe?

The army marched on to Glorieta continuing to show its strength. The Battle of Glorieta was going badly for the Union Army. The immediate aim of the Confederate forces was to take Fort Union and then go north into Colorado.

335. How did the Union forces turn the tide at Glorieta?

In a brilliant move, Chaves of the Colorado Volunteers led Major Chivington's group over rugged terrain behind enemy lines and destroyed a supply train of more than sixty wagons and killed about a thousand mules. Without food, arms and other supplies, the Confederate army could not continue to fight so they beat a quick retreat down the Rio Grande.

336. What was the third battle in New Mexico?

At Peralta, just south of Albuquerque, the third battle of the Civil War was fought. Canby and his soldiers, angered at having been forced by the powerful and fully equipped Confederate Army to seek refuge in Fort Craig, were spoiling for a battle. It was more of a chase than a battle. The rebels were heading toward El Paso with Canby's men on their heels.

337. What did the Confederate forces then do?

The rebels sued for a truce and buried their dead, thus ending the war in New Mexico. In about a year of fighting, around thirteen hundred men were killed with no territorial gains for the Confederate Army.

338. How was the commander at Glorieta rewarded?

For his part in the victory at Glorieta, John Chivington was promoted to colonel. He remained with the Colorado Volunteers for the rest of the war and led the infamous and controversial attack on Black Kettle, a Cheyenne chief, at Sand Creek in November 1864.

339. What happened to General Sibley after his defeat?

On the Confederate side, Henry Sibley left the country after the war and tried to help the Khedive of Egypt organize an army. His attempts were unsuccessful due to mismanagement and his continuing penchant for the bottle. Finally he returned to Fredericksburg, Virginia where he died penniless in 1886.

340. Why was Glorieta so important?

The Battle of Glorieta is sometimes called the "Gettysburg of the West" because it was a decisive battle of the Civil War.

341. How do Santa Feans relate the Sena Plaza with the Civil War?

As a footnote to the Civil War, Santa Feans enjoy an old square called "Sena Plaza." Jose Sena, a major on the side of the Union forces during the Civil War, inherited this property from his mother. Ownership goes back to the time when Don Diego de Vargas gave the property as a land grant to Captain Arias de Quiros.

342. How did Jose Sena improve the property?

Jose Sena expanded the property from a small house to a very large thirty-three-room hacienda, to house twenty-three children. Originally the ground floor had no openings to the streets except a large wagon passageway on the north side of the plaza. Today it is a popular meeting place for dining and listening to music.

343. Why are there so few historical records in Santa Fe?

In 1870, a territorial governor who had scant visibility or success in his functions as the chief civil administrator of New Mexico decided to enter the history books by reason of stupidity. William Pile sold the Spanish archives stored in the Palace of the Governors as scrap paper, destroying most of the documents from the Spanish Colonial and Mexican periods.

19

Kit Carson

344. Who was Kit Carson?

Of all the mountain men who came to New Mexico, Kit Carson had the most impact on the future of the territory.

345. What were his origins?

Christopher Houston Carson was born in 1809, on Christmas Eve in Kentucky. He lost his father when he was only nine years old and for lack of money, Chris had to drop out of school. To earn money, he learned the trade of saddle making. At the first opportunity, the boy joined a wagon train that was going to Santa Fe.

346. How did Kit Carson spend the first years in the West?

During the first few years, Kit Carson lived part of the time in Taos and spent part of his time fur trapping throughout the West. In the 1840s, he worked for a while as a hunter for William Bent at Bent's Fort. He became fluent in Indian languages and integrated himself fully into the world of the Indian. His first two wives were Arapaho and Cheyenne.

347. When did the difficulties with the various Indian tribes reach unbearable levels?

During the war in New Mexico, the Comanche, Apache and Navaho made trouble by raiding the settlements. Both sides claimed the other had broken the truce. In September 1862, General James Carleton succeeded Canby as commander of the Military Department. He made plans for solving the Indian problem.

348. How did General Carleton begin to solve the Indian problem?

The Mescalero Apache were to be dealt with first. Carleton engaged Colonel Kit Carson to move about four hundred warriors and their families to Bosque Redondo in the valley of the Pecos River where they were to be held until decisions could be made about their future. The troops at Fort Sumner were to guard the Apache.

349. How did Carleton deal with the Navaho Indians?

The Navaho question was more complex. The peaceful Navaho Indians were to be separated from the hostile ones. Those who would be willing to be separated were sent to Bosque Redondo. Carleton met with the Navaho leaders and told them their word had been broken too many times and that the army would use force to control them. Kit Carson had the unpleasant task of going to Canyon de Chelly to show the Navaho population that the army meant business.

350. What was Kit Carson's response to this plan?

Carson was opposed to the plan for demanding unconditional surrender of the Navaho or face extermination. He attempted to be relieved of his duties but was unsuccessful. The hostile Navaho would not cooperate and would not surrender. It was in the last months of 1863 that Carson's troops marched through the Navaho homeland.

351. What specific mission did Carson and his men receive?

Their mission was to destroy all Navaho sources of food supply—their crops and stores were burned, fruit trees destroyed and livestock captured. The starving Indians were at last willing to comply with the demands of General Carleton—obey rather than be put to death. Carson led the Navaho to the reservation at Bosque Redondo. The Navaho refer to this displacement at the "Long Walk."

352. Why was this displacement project unsuccessful?

The Bosque Redondo project was doomed for failure. The Apache and Navaho were not compatible. The hope that the tribes would soon become self-sufficient was, as well, unrealized. Soon afterward, the Navaho were allowed to return to their homeland; the Apache broke away and disappeared into the hills.

353. How can one characterize the mood of the inhabitants of the capital after the war?

After the Civil War, the territory and its capital, Santa Fe suffered a period of general lawlessness. In one month, three murders were committed near the plaza in addition to countless beatings. Few men were willing to risk their lives to become sheriffs or deputies. Soldiers of the cavalry were spending more time chasing thieves than in fighting Indians.

354. What happened to Chief Justice Slough?

One example of lawlessness was the slaying of John P. Slough, Chief Justice of the Territorial Supreme Court. Slough, had originally arrived in New Mexico with the Colorado volunteers during the Civil War. In 1867, he was gunned down in La Fonda Hotel by William L. Rynerson on the pretext that Slough had reached for his derringer first."

355. Why was there so much lawlessness?

Lawlessness existed in the Southwest for several reasons. There was little homogeneity among the citizens who traveled to Santa Fe after New Mexico became a Mexican province in 1821. The law that applied there was not made for the conditions that existed and was unsuitable for those conditions. Since it was perceived that no one could enforce the law, each man had to make his own law and usually he enforced it with his six-shooter.

356. What took the place of law?

In the absence of law in the social conditions that prevailed, men worked out an extra-legal code that demanded fair play. For example, one must never shoot an adversary in the back or shoot an unarmed man.

357. In what other way did the population of Santa Fe prove to be unruly?

In addition to crime, the citizens had grown careless with their garbage. Water Street today was once an open sewer where dead animals and refuse of every sort floated. The police posted a ruling, which read: "Every house owner or head of family within the limits of the city of Santa Fe shall specially take care that his servants or attendants do not throw dirty water, rubbish, ashes or kitchen offal in the public squares, roads, streets or lanes of the City."

20

The Railroad

358. What did the coming of the railroad mean to the people of New Mexico?

Although there was some ambivalence concerning the coming of the railroad to New Mexico, most of the population viewed it with excited anticipation.

359. What were the diverse attitudes toward the railroad?

Those in favor said it meant more tourism and more trade, which meant more prosperity. The traditionalists were concerned that the railroad would bring an undesirable element of society. In the 1870s, as the railroad began to cross Kansas, the fervor grew. The Santa Fe Trail had been the only connection with the East and trade had been brisk.

360. How successful had the Santa Fe Trail been prior to the arrival of the railroad?

After the end of the Civil War, there were fewer problems with the Indians. The Trail was carrying unprecedented weight in goods, much of it military cargo for the new forts.

361. How were the citizens of Santa Fe cautioned about the railroad?

The railroad promised to increase the capacity of cargo a hundred fold. *The New Mexican* cautioned its readers: "The citizens of Santa Fe must themselves show some measure of confidence in the city if they expect railroads and manufactures and commercial men to show confidence in a town and come here and invest their capital."

362. What did the railroad companies expect from the communities they served?

The commercial entities of Santa Fe were urged to raise money to support the coming railroad. The railroad companies expected established communities to subsidize the construction of their lines. After all, it would be these communities that would benefit financially from the increased trade.

363. How did Santa Fe react to being asked to pay?

Initially, Santa Fe reacted badly to the proposal that the city had to help pay for the railroad. Agents from the Denver and Rio Grande Railroad were sent packing. Clearly the leading citizens had to get used to the idea.

364. What were the concerns of the railroad at this juncture?

Another problem that was unforeseen earlier was the fact that the railroads had had a relatively easy time crossing the plains of Kansas. When the railroad made it into Colorado, especially the mountains around Raton Pass, the owners saw that each mile in rough terrain would cost many additional dollars.

365. What did the leaders of Santa Fe decide and how was their decision viewed?

City leaders, fearing that Santa Fe might be bypassed altogether by the railroad, made contact with the Atchison, Topeka and Santa Fe (AT&SF) Company. Meanwhile, the engineers projecting the path of the railroad advised that Santa Fe be bypassed altogether. Their reasons were sound—to leave the flat land to bring the railroad to an altitude of seven thousand feet just to include the capital of New Mexico made no sense.

366. What finally happened?

The residents of Santa Fe were disappointed. At last a bond issue was approved for $150,000 to have an eighteen-mile spur line join Santa Fe to the main line at a town named after Archbishop Lamy. The first train arrived in Santa Fe in April, 1880; it was an excursion train for celebrating the opening of a new era.

367. What did the labor force consist of?

The labor force on the railroad was at first mainly Irish. Soon New Mexicans were hired as well as Asians and even some Indians. All along the line, new towns began springing up. Opportunity arose for those who wanted to prepare food for the passengers at the various stops.

368. Who initially benefited from the railroad?

Las Vegas, New Mexico was one of the first towns to benefit from the arrival of the railroad in 1879. The city shipped out in one year ten million dollars worth of hides, wool and pelts.

369. How did the railway further benefit from the line?

The AT&SF started to build hotels along its line. In Santa Fe, the location where La Fonda presently stands was the Exchange Hotel—an establishment for clients of the railway. One story relates that Billy the Kid once washed dishes in the Exchange Hotel.

370. When did the Exchange Hotel become La Fonda?

In 1919, the Exchange Hotel was demolished. The present-day La Fonda was built a year later on the same site. In 1926, La Fonda became a part of the Harvey House hotel chain and remained one for more than forty years.

371. In what other ways did the railway encourage growth?

The railroad permitted the transportation of heavy machinery, which allowed more lumber and stone to be processed locally. Railroad companies energetically promoted settlement along the western routes, luring prospective homesteaders with pictures of bountiful fields, prosperous farmers and easy rewards. The black community of Nicodemus, Kansas for example, owed its existence to such boosterism. Handbills were distributed that said: "All Colored People that want to go TO KANSAS, on September 5, 1877, can do so for $5.00."

372. What was the result of this type of effort?

The railroad was allowing the West to be populated. The Homestead Act of 1862 gave impetus to this movement. The Homestead Act with its amendments increased the size of a land grant from 160 acres to 640 acres and a shortened period of compulsory residence.

373. What unsavory types took advantage of this population explosion?

The stagecoach robbers of the Santa Fe Trail naturally often became train robbers in the 1880s. In a small New Mexican town, the following sign was posted near the railroad station: "Notice to Thieves, Thugs, Fakirs and Bunkosteerers: If found within the limits of this city after Ten O'clock PM, this night, you will be invited to attend a Grand Neck-Tie Party, the expense of which will be borne by 100 SUBSTANTIAL CITIZENS."

374. How successful were these railway robbers?

Robbing passengers on rail coaches succeeded only part of the time. In the annals of the railway, most robbers were either shot in the act or jailed when the train reached the next depot.

21

Governor Lew Wallace

375. Who was Lew Wallace?

The man who was to become the 97th governor since Western colonization, Lew Wallace, was unique. He was the son of an Indiana governor, an ex-Civil War hero and the author of a successful novel about the life of Jesus Christ—*Ben-Hur*.

376. Why is Lew Wallace not generally known to this generation?

Besides having a building and a school named after him, he is today relatively unknown. In his time, however, he was very popular. His published books earned him more royalties than any American novelist before him.

377. What were the concerns of society during the 1880s?

Author William Barrett compares the concerns of the 21st Century governor to those of the 1880s. He says: "Present-day New Mexico has high crime, not enough prisons, Indian conflicts and an activist governor warring with legislators and judges. Just like back in 1880."

378. What were Lew Wallace's priorities upon taking office?

When Wallace arrived in Santa Fe, he already knew his priority would be law and order. There was a run of crimes that were quite serious—murder of prominent citizens, rape and grand theft.

379. What was the Lincoln County War about?

The Lincoln County War was mistakenly labeled a range war—involving disputes of the cattle market, but in truth it was a blood feud.

380. How did Governor Wallace get involved?

Billy the Kid got involved on the side of one of the factions and drew so much attention that Governor Wallace went to Lincoln County in southern New Mexico to investigate the situation.

381. Who were the opposing sides of this feud?

Alexander McSween bought an interest in a ranch and built a store to challenge the opposing interest of businessman Lawrence Murphy who had a trade monopoly in the area. On the side of McSween was an Englishman named John Henry Tunstall. In the first exchange of gunfire of the Lincoln County War, Tunstall was gunned down in cold blood.

382. How did Billy the Kid get involved?

Enter William "Billy the Kid" Bonney who took the side of the dead Tunstall and had the two gunmen responsible for the killing murdered.

383. What did Governor Wallace do?

It was in the midst of this convoluted situation that Governor Wallace found himself. In order to get sufficient information, Wallace personally negotiated with and promised clemency to, the murderer, Billy the Kid. The deal, however, fell through and Billy the Kid was convicted of murder.

384. When did Governor Wallace become disenchanted with his job?

Governor Wallace grew disillusioned with his work and in March 1881, he approached the new President Garfield and submitted his resignation. On leaving his post, he said to a group of friends: "At least I haven't been jailed or murdered...." Before leaving New Mexico, in a letter to his wife he wrote: "I have spent enough time in this place. There is nobody who cares for me and nobody I care for."

385. What did Mrs. Wallace say to show her disdain for New Mexico?

Susan Wallace, the governor's wife is quoted as saying: "We should have another war with Old Mexico to make her take back New Mexico."

22

Billy the Kid

386. What did Billy the Kid look like?

It's unfortunate that the only available photograph of Billy the Kid makes him out to be less of a hero than our imagination might require. In the photo, he is standing with his rifle at his side. He appears to be narrow at the shoulder and wide at the hips and his face appears to be irregularly shaped.

387. What was his real name?

He had several names: "Henry McCarty," "William H. Bonney" and "The Kid."

388. Who were Billy's parents?

His parents were Catherine and Michael McCarty—immigrants from poverty-stricken Ireland and its famine. When Billy's mother died of tuberculosis about nine years after she had married Billy's stepfather, the boy was pretty much on his own.

389. How old was Billy when he started to break the law?

At fourteen, he fell in with a rough element, did odd jobs and learned how to steal for a living.

390. How old was Billy the Kid when he first murdered a man?

In front of witnesses in a saloon in Fort Grant, Arizona Territory, Billy killed his first person (at least that we know of). In an argument with a blacksmith named "Cahill," Billy drew his pistol and shot the man dead. He was an outlaw at seventeen.

391. How were Billy and John Tunstall involved?

Billy served as a ranch hand for a wealthy Englishman—John Henry Tunstall. When Tunstall was killed, Billy and his gang called the "Regulators" killed the two men responsible for Tunstall's death.

392. During what period was Billy living in Fort Sumner?

From 1878–1880, Billy was in Fort Sumner. He had been rustling cattle and had managed to remain on the loose. Billy was wanted for the killing of Sheriff Brady as well. During the Lincoln County War, he added two more notches to his gun. Pat Garrett, the sheriff of Lincoln County vowed to capture the Kid.

393. When did Pat Garrett capture Billy?

Garrett captured Billy in December 1880 and two of Billy's sidekicks were shot. Billy's attitude was such that he believed he was invincible. He was tried in Mesilla, convicted of several murders and sentenced to hang.

394. What happened next?

The Kid was being held in a second-story room of the courthouse. He was one month away from being hanged. On April 18, 1881, Billy escaped by killing his two guards. Billy left Lincoln County and went to Fort Sumner where he hid for a couple of months.

395. When was Billy the Kid killed?

On July 14, 1881, Garrett located the fugitive and shot him in the heart. Billy the Kid was twenty-one years old and ironically had twenty-one notches in his gun.

396. Do we know when Billy the Kid stayed in Santa Fe?

Two stories about Billy place him in Santa Fe—one as a dishwasher at the hotel now called La Fonda, the other as he was being pursued by the posse down Agua Fria road.

397. What happened to Pat Garrett?

As a footnote to history, Garrett was shot and killed by Wayne Brazil over a lease on Garrett's ranch that Brazil held. The year was 1908.

23

Geronimo

398. What was occurring in Santa Fe at the time Lew Wallace left his position?

Lionel A. Sheldon succeeded Lew Wallace as governor of New Mexico in 1881. Among his concerns, which were many, was the Apache Indian problem. In May of 1885, the last year of Sheldon's tenure as governor, the Apache fled the San Carlos reservation in Arizona.

399. Who led the Apache in their escape?

Under the leadership of Mangus Chihuahua and the shaman Geronimo, the "hostiles" headed for the open spaces, which were so dear to these semi-nomads.

400. What was life on the reservation like for the Apache?

Life on the San Carlos reservation had been difficult and confining for the Apache. If the nature of the Apache had been to live and let live, the history of this people would have been written differently. The Apache, however, were warlike and wreaked destruction in their path.

401. How large was the band that had escaped from the reservation?

The band consisted of thirty-five men, eight boys and about one hundred women and children.

402. How long would these Apache remain free?

Over a period of sixteen months, they would remain free while five thousand troops and many Indian auxiliaries would try to round them up. During that time, the Apache killed seventy-five citizens and several officers and soldiers of the regular army.

403. Who was in charge of capturing Geronimo?

General Crook established a command post in Fort Bayard, New Mexico. After months of rumors of the whereabouts of the hostiles, months of indignant telegrams with Washington, the army closed in on Geronimo and his group who had fled to Mexico.

404. When were Geronimo and his band captured?

In mid-July of 1886, Lieutenant Charles Gatewood crossed into Mexico from New Mexico. More than a month later, he picked up the trail of the Apache. He met the hostiles on the banks of the Bavispe River and urged them to surrender. On September 3rd, Geronimo and his followers agreed to terms and were taken into custody.

24

Education and Growth in the 19th Century

405. How was church-oriented education viewed in the 19th Century?

With the impetus given by Archbishop Lamy for the establishment of a school for boys under the Christian Brothers and a school for girls under the Sisters of Loretto and the Sisters of Charity, there was strong interest for continued growth of church-sponsored education during the rest of the century throughout the state.

406. What schools were established at this time?

The Jesuits established St. Mary's School in Albuquerque in 1893, which was run as a coeducational parochial institution. St. Catherine's Industrial Indian School of Santa Fe was founded in 1886 by the Archbishop Salpointe and Mother Catherine Drexel of Philadelphia. In 1888, the Christian Brothers founded the La Salle Institute at Las Vegas, New Mexico and maintained it until 1927.

407. What advances did the Protestants make?

Protestant groups were also active in developing schools in the mid 1800s. The Presbyterian Church established a day school at Laguna Pueblo in 1866. Under Reverend Harwood, the Methodist Church made its first steps in education in 1871. The Congregational Church came to Santa Fe in 1878.

408. What attempts were made for public schools?

With illiteracy marked at over seventy-five percent, there were early attempts to create free public schools. It was, however, not until 1891 that a law was passed to provide for a Territorial Board of Education. A tax levy was put into place with the proceeds given to the districts.

409. Was public school voluntary?

At first, there was little concern about this. Attendance at school became mandatory between the ages of eight and sixteen for a minimum of three months per year.

410. How did language play a role in education?

The problems of bilingual instruction in public schools were gradually reduced. As employment opportunities grew and travel outside the state became more common, New Mexicans had more contact with Anglo populations and were able to learn to improve their knowledge of English.

411. When was higher education available in New Mexico?

In 1892, higher education came to New Mexico. The Territorial Legislature established several schools. The University of New Mexico began its classes that year in Albuquerque.

25

19th Century Leaders

412. Who was Thomas B. Catron?

One of the first U.S. Senators for New Mexico was a Republican—Thomas B. Catron who arrived in New Mexico in 1866 after serving in the Confederate Army. "Boss" Catron was determined to make himself rich.

413. How did he go about making money?

As a lawyer, he dedicated himself to the complicated business of sorting out the land grant problems. As an expert on land grants, he made a fortune for himself and managed to acquire vast expanses of land.

414. What other business deals was he involved in?

He was a director and major shareholder in cattle corporations that owned the southern half of Santa Fe County as well as most of what is now Catron County. At one time or another, he gained an interest or clear title in 34 land grants, totaling three million acres.

415. What ethical criticisms did he face?

A good many of the people he represented were illiterate and could not read the documents he had them sign. He was accused of being unprofessional and corrupt but he was too clever to suffer from these accusations.

416. How successful was Catron in politics?

As a politician, he practically ran the Republican Party single-handedly. He was the acknowledged leader of the Santa Fe Ring—a group of hard-line politically astute businessmen.

417. What marked the start of Catron's decline?

With the appointment of Miguel Otero, Jr., as territorial governor in 1897, Catron's power began to diminish. Men such as Catron grew rich through tactics that would be illegal today but this was widespread in the American West during the "robber baron" era.

418. How did Governor Otero get started in politics?

His first job was that of a bookkeeper and he entered politics in 1883 as City Treasurer of Las Vegas. After working in several clerk positions in various court offices, he got involved with the Republican Party and was appointed Territorial Governor in 1897.

419. Where was Governor Otero originally from?

Miguel A. Otero, Jr. was born in St. Louis Missouri, October 17, 1849. His parents returned to their permanent home in New Mexico when the boy was two years old. He received a religious education at a local school— Notre Dame.

420. What did Otero accuse certain U.S. Senators of doing as a result of his bid for New Mexican statehood?

He accused certain junketing senators, ostensibly coming to New Mexico to gather positive information about the territory, of cementing their preconceived opinions and to further gather negative data.

421. What accusations did Otero make of Senator L.G. Rothchild?

"He would sneak around the slum districts and meet impossible people in order to make an adverse report on conditions as found by him. Absolutely not the slightest attention was paid to the favorable side of the territory, and no inquiry was made covering education, industry, manufacturing, banking, stock-raising, mining or farming."

422. How did the Spanish-American War help New Mexico in its bid for statehood?

In 1898, Congress declared war against Spain in an attempt to help Cuba win its independence from that country. The question asked was whether New Mexico would join in the fight against its first mother country. The response was resoundingly affirmative.

423. What did the war achieve for Miguel Otero?

Miguel A. Otero, Jr., the first Hispanic governor since 1846, had the distinction of serving the longest period in that capacity as part of the United States. The war had a short duration—six months and the United States achieved all its aims.

424. How did the New Mexicans respond to the call to war?

With the outbreak of the war, the governor called for volunteers and the response was overwhelming.

425. Who was Miguel Antonio Otero?

He was Governor Otero's father. Miguel Antonio Otero was a major contributor to the economic development of New Mexico. He was seated as a Territorial Delegate to the U.S. House of Representatives in 1856 and with the support of Bishop Lamy was reelected to the next two Congresses. When Otero senior completed his terms in Congress, he was considered for the post of Minister to Spain. President Lincoln believed Otero was exceptionally qualified. Otero, however, declined the office.

26

Lifestyle in the 19th Century

426. What did the average Anglo-American think of New Mexico?

With the Santa Fe Trail and later with the railroads, Anglo-Americans flooded into New Mexico. Their initial appraisal of the territory was uniformly negative.

427. What was their major complaint?

They felt that they had stepped back in time and had found none of the modern conveniences they were used to and thought they needed. Much of what was prevalent in 16th Century Spain still existed in 19th Century New Mexico.

428. What more was the average Anglo disappointed with?

The society included a few very wealthy people but most of the people had to struggle hard for just an existence. The Church had as much a hold on its congregation as it did in Medieval Europe.

429. What might the visitors from the United States say about the roads or the construction of homes?

The roads were poorly maintained, the houses were constructed with any materials that could be found. There seemed to be little order in the life of the inhabitants.

430. What might have been their first impression of the Palace of the Governors?

Those visitors who had heard about the Palace of the Governors before coming to Santa Fe were exceptionally disappointed by the long, low-slung building, constructed it seemed from the very mud of the narrow lanes that surrounded it.

431. How had the mud construction changed with the arrival of the Spaniards?

The "puddle adobe"—the simple way the Indians had poured wet mud and waited for it to dry before pouring more—was improved upon by the Spaniards who taught the Indians how to form bricks and stack the walls of their houses.

432. How were individual homes built?

Visitors in the 19th Century saw that little change had taken place in this construction since the conquistadors. The houses were built, as many had been built in Spain with a small patio in the middle of the area with several rooms opening to it. No openings were placed on the outside of the house, for reasons of security. For the most part, floors were of earth, sometimes treated to give them a hardened surface. The roofs were flat and could not prevent the rain from coming into the rooms.

433. How were the homes heated?

Usually one room had a fireplace lit all the time. This was often the kitchen where the family gathered to eat and do whatever chores they could. The bedrooms were not heated. The bedding, however, was heated with hot coals prior to retiring for the night. Candles were made at home and used sparingly.

434. How were the walls of the houses finished?

Similar to the custom in Spain, women used a lime and chalk mixture to cover the walls making them white. This surface did not last long and, as a rule, had to be redone every year.

435. How were the homes furnished?

Furniture was sparse, even among the wealthy. Beds were rare, only mattresses were thrown on the floor at night. These mattresses were stuffed with straw and often some sweet-smelling herbs. Valuables were kept in trunks—usually made of rawhide. Kitchen utensils were usually made of earthenware and had multiple uses during the meal.

436. How did New Mexicans dress at this period?

New Mexicans wore clothing that provided warmth and they did not change as often as we, in this century, would prefer. Clothing was homemade with close-fitting buckskin to keep out the cold. The women used scent to compensate for and cover up odors that came from fireplace smoke and perspiration.

437. What about female clothing?

Despite the poverty in which most of the people lived, there was that pride in appearance for the men and a bit of the coquette in the women. The women would wear a "rebozo"—a long scarf up to six feet long that was thrown over the shoulders and dangled to the waist. It served as a bonnet, a shawl, an apron and a bodice.

438. How were men normally dressed?

Men wore their sombrero—a word that comes from the Spanish word, "sombra" meaning "shade." An all-purpose garment for the men was the serape, which was slung over the shoulders and could serve as an overcoat, raincoat or blanket.

439. What kind of recreation did the New Mexicans provide for themselves?

With the permission of the Church, dances were frequently held on fiesta days. Sponsored often by the Church, these dances were carefully monitored. The instruments that accompanied the dance were the violin and the guitar. A good deal of thumping was a sign that the dance was unusually successful. The strict behavior of the New Mexican was sometimes disturbed by the arrival of the Anglo who liked to drink alcohol at the dances.

440. Did the Church permit gambling?

Despite the prohibition of the friars, gambling was ever-present in New Mexico. Horse racing and cock fighting were common and betting always made the action interesting. At one time, Santa Fe had sixty licensed gambling places. With the coming of the soldiers and the building of Fort Marcy, gambling reached its peak.

441. What were the attitudes toward sex at this period?

While the Puritans of the East of an earlier period were restrained in matters of sex, available records show that premarital sex in New Mexico was widely tolerated in the 19th Century but marital infidelities were severely punished. The Church, of course, strongly forbade this behavior.

442. What other entertainment did the Church sanction?

The Church sponsored the plays that depicted the important moments in the lives of Christ and the Virgin Mary. These plays were often held on the grounds of the church and performed during the holy days. Because the people were predominantly illiterate, the play became a means of education. Sometimes the plays depicted important events in Spanish history like the battle between the Christians and the Moors.

443. Was physical exercise permitted?

Physical exercise was encouraged but not at the cost of sin. As late as April 26, 1877, the attorney general, in support of the Church's wishes, proclaimed that all persons engaging in playing baseball on Sunday were guilty of a violation of the "Sunday Law." These people were liable to prosecution and punishment.

27

Statehood for New Mexico

444. When did New Mexico first apply for statehood?

From the time New Mexico attained its status as a U.S. Territory, it began to petition for statehood. Between 1849 and 1910, fifty acts were introduced for statehood. Just as quickly, New Mexico was denied these requests by the U.S. Congress.

445. Why were these requests denied?

At first, the reason was the slavery issue; later it was because of the antagonism over Reconstruction. Perhaps greater than these excuses were these two: religious bigotry and racial discrimination. Anglo-Americans did not really accept that New Mexico was a part of the United States.

446. How did language and culture play a part in these decisions?

The Congress reasoned that the language was not English; the culture was foreign; and the Catholic Church was much too powerful.

447. Were all New Mexicans interested in becoming Americans?

Behind the scenes were those New Mexicans who did not want statehood but would not speak out against it. These were the great landowners and large merchants who were afraid they would have to pay much higher taxes as part of the Union.

448. How often did this territory petition for statehood?

Between December 1891 and June 1903, no fewer than 20 bills were introduced to admit New Mexico to statehood. Only three passed the House and then died. Easterners were afraid the West would become too powerful and they also feared having more pro-silver clout in the Senate.

449. How did the Rough Riders help the cause for New Mexican statehood?

In a peculiar way, the Spanish-American War did some good for the cause of statehood. More of Theodore Roosevelt's Rough Riders came from New Mexico and Arizona than any other area. After the war, Theodore Roosevelt kept in touch with many of his Rough Riders. Their first reunion was held in Las Vegas, New Mexico in June 1899. While there, Roosevelt pledged himself for statehood, saying: "All I shall say is if New Mexico wants to be a state, you can count me in, and I will go back to Washington to speak for you or do anything you wish."

450. What events took place to make Roosevelt forget his promise to help?

On his way out to the West Coast, President McKinley was assassinated while stopping at Deming, New Mexico in May 1901. The leader of the Rough Riders, then Vice-President became President of the United States. To the disappointment of the people of the state, President Theodore Roosevelt did not follow through on his promise.

451. What proposals were then made concerning New Mexico and Arizona?

Because statehood for New Mexico had been so elusive a goal, the next step was to attempt to bring New Mexico and Arizona in jointly as one state. This proposal would clearly satisfy some of the easterners who feared too much power would be accumulated in the west.

452. What reasons were given for Arizona to oppose this jointure?

In the spring of 1902, it looked like it would be jointure or nothing. Most of the folks from Arizona were against this proposal. They argued that the people of the two territories were quite different. New Mexicans had a strong Mexican background while this was not true of Arizona. Besides, Arizona was reluctant to put its considerable mining interests under the control of Santa Fe. New Mexico, in contrast, favored jointure.

453. What did Congress finally decide?

A bill came to a vote for jointure but was defeated. It was not until 1912 that New Mexico entered the Union as the forty-seventh state followed by Arizona, the same year, as the forty-eighth state.

454. When did this decision formally become law?

More than a century of national expansion culminated on February 14, 1912 when President William Howard Taft signed the long-awaited proclamation. This was also the year that Alaska was granted territorial status in the United States.

455. How did statehood change the people of New Mexico?

In the years that followed the proclamation of statehood, the people of New Mexico began more and more to integrate themselves with the rest of the nation. Growing pains were evident but the West was open for business.

28

Modern Times

456. What problems of the past no longer troubled New Mexico?

No longer were the Indians creating problems for the inhabitants (though we may have a different view of the struggle today than we did in the time of Kit Carson). No longer did France, Spain or Mexico lay claim to the Southwest (although Pancho Villa raided Columbus, New Mexico in 1916).

457. How did the attitude of out-of-state visitors change?

No longer did visitors come to Santa Fe expecting to see what they had left in their hometowns, the same kind of lifestyle or the same kind of Anglo building construction. Above all, no longer did the visitors want to see New Mexico copy what was taking place in the East.

458. What did the Santa Fean and the visitor learn to prize in the city?

A new and genuine appreciation grew for the ancient city. Even a "Styles Ordinance" had for its primary goal to recreate the look of adobe in the center of town. The tourist wanted to see what was old—the older the better. Although the American tourists still flock to Europe to see the old cathedrals and plazas, they have a certain pride in knowing that their own Santa Fe boasts a similar heritage.

459. What efforts were made in architecture?

Among the architects to come to Santa Fe from Colorado was Isaac H. Rapp. He had an innovative spirit and did not mind experimenting. His attempt at creating a Santa Fe Style ended up looking more like California Revival. About the time the Old Palace was being remodeled by Nusbaum, Rapp built the Scottish Rite Temple in the city, modeled after the famous gate of the Alhambra in Granada, Spain.

460. What drew artists to Santa Fe?

Artists came to Santa Fe for a multitude of reasons. In 1917, the Museum of Fine Arts was dedicated. That same year, Georgia O'Keeffe visited the state for the first time. Writers came for the sense of openness and creative freedom; painters came for the light; and tourists came for everything they could see or buy. Some like John Gaw Meem initially came because of a respiratory illness and stayed to make a lasting impression on the architecture of the city.

461. What important project did New Mexico undertake during the Second World War?

During the Second World War, Los Alamos took its place on the international stage with the creation of the Manhattan Project. Some of the greatest scientific minds in the world were invited to New Mexico to create the atomic bomb. Today, it takes a sleuth of exceptional ability to find the plaque designating the administrative office of the Manhattan Project among the antiques and flowers on Palace Avenue in Santa Fe.

462. What was the Miracle in the Desert?

In 1957, The Santa Fe Opera opened and was called the "Miracle in the Desert."

463. How were Indian artists recognized for their contributions?

American Indian artists were encouraged with the establishment by Executive Order under President Kennedy in 1962 of the Institute of American Indian Arts (IAIA) formerly known under a much longer title.

464. What other reasons do tourists have for visiting Santa Fe?

Today, thousands of visitors come to Santa Fe for the music, the theatre, the museums, the scores of galleries, for the Spanish and Indian Markets and for a sojourn into the past. In 1998, New Mexico celebrated its cuartocentenario—four hundred years of existence. Those of us who call

Santa Fe home are proud of what our city was in the past and what it has, over the years, become. And the visitors, who are always among us, seem to be delighted by the city's history, its culture and its charm.

Conclusion

To say that the questions I have chosen to ask in this book are the most important ones would be too simplistic. The number of queries about any subject are infinite. Perhaps 501 or even 1001 would have been better, but maybe only slightly. My point is that I have scratched the surface of a subject that I hope will entice you to read further into the history of this remarkable city and state. Again, to emphasize, as I have done, certain aspects of Santa Fe's history and that of New Mexico, to the exclusion of others, is merely my choice. A somewhat more enhanced treatment of this topic can be found in my book: *Old Santa Fe – A Brief Review of History*. Should you already have a good basic knowledge of the history of America's Southwest and would enjoy a tongue-in-cheek version of events, you may want to read another one of my books: *Pulling No Ponchos – An Irreverent History of Santa Fe*. Both titles have been published by Sunstone Press.

Needless to say there are many excellent studies published in books and journals, which treat in much more detail the origins of Spanish exploration of New Mexico, the goals of the conquistadores, the conflict with Native Americans, the Civil War in New Mexico, etc.

My efforts here have been modest. I simply wanted to focus on aspects of the life and culture of the people who inhabited these lands and those of the people who came seeking fame and wealth but stayed to leave a lasting mark on customs, language and religion.

The reader might find it curious that so little has changed in regards to religious tolerance from the sixteen hundreds to the present. As a global society, we are still convinced that our version of the truth is the only genuine version. We still scorn those who do not believe as we do, call them infidels or try to enlist them to support our views. One has only to travel the world to see the hundreds of different expressions of faith to be convinced that wherever devotion manifests itself, it should be embraced, provided it causes no harm. And those who wish to be free from all religious ties should not be persecuted. We see time and time again how churches become powerful and seek to use their strength to influence the laws of the land. We have seen it with the Catholic Church during many centuries and we see it among many of our Protestant denominations today in our own country. Separation of church and state may be an ideal but we, in fact, have not yet embraced it in reality.

As a nation, we still have a long way to go in accepting group diversity as well as individual differences of our people. The fact is that Santa Fe is this nation's oldest capital; yet, New Mexico was one of the last states to attain statehood is troublesome. I would hope that the motives for denying statehood for so many years are not still alive in the minds of our nation's leaders who may view Native or Spanish origins to be less American and therefore worthy of less consideration. As a nation, we must one day come to terms with the reality that our methods in the past of expanding our borders were not without serious blemish; however we may try to justify them. As a nation, we must stop basing our foreign policy on the acquisition of riches for the few, rather than on genuine human values. One day we may earn the true place of leader among the community of nations. Through greed, Spain lost Florida, Louisiana and the entire Southwest. There may be a lesson here for us at only fourteen years into the 21st Century.

Further Reading

Abbink, Emily. *New Mexico's Palace of the Governors: History of an American Treasure*. Santa Fe: Museum of New Mexico Press, 2007

Dary, David. *The Santa Fe Trail: Its History, Legends, and Lore*. New York: Knopf, 2001.

Fugate, Francis L. and Roberta B. *Roadside History of New Mexico*. Missoula, MT: Mountain Press Publishing Company, 1989.

Gregg, Josiah. *Gregg's Commerce of the Prairies or the journal of a Santa Fe Trader, 1831–1839*. Carlisle, MA: Applewood Books, 2007.rio

Harris, Richard. *The National Trust Guide to Santa Fe: America's Guide for Architecture and History Travelers*. New York: Wiley, 1997.

Hyslop, Stephen G. *Bound for Santa Fe: The Road to New Mexico and the American Conquest, 1806–1848*. Norman: University of Oklahoma Press, 2002.

Jaehn, Tomas. *Germans in the Southwest, 1850–1920*. Albuquerque: The University of New Mexico Press, 2005.

———. *Jewish Pioneers of New Mexico*. Santa Fe: Museum of New Mexico Press, 2004.

———. Translator, Editor, and Annotator. *T he Pastor of New Mexico, Peter Küppers's Memoirs*. Santa Fe: Sunstone Press, 2014

Lummis, Charles F. *The Land of Poco Tiempo*. Albuquerque: The University of New Mexico Press, 1966.

Weber, David J. *The Spanish Frontier in North America*. New Haven: Yale University Press, 1992.

Books on Santa Fe and New Mexico from Sunstone Press
(As of 2015)

All Trails Lead to Santa Fe: An Anthology Commemorating the 400th Anniversary of the Founding of Santa Fe, New Mexico, in 1610. Santa Fe: Sunstone Press, 2010.

Aragón, Ray John de. *The Penitentes of New Mexico: Hermanos de la Luz / Brothers of the Light*. Santa Fe, Sunstone Press, 2006.

———. *The Legend of La Llorona*. Santa Fe: Sunstone Press, 2006.

Aranda, Charles. *Dichos: Proverbs and Sayings from the Spanish*. Santa Fe: Sunstone Press, 1977.

Austin, Mary Hunter. *Earth Horizon*. Facsimile of 1932 edition. Santa Fe: Sunstone Press, 2007.

———. *Land of Little Rain*. Facsimile of 1904 edition. Santa Fe: Sunstone Press, 2007.

Bullock, Alice. *Discover Santa Fe*. Santa Fe: Rydal Press, distributed by Sunstone Press, 1973.

———. *Living Legends of the Santa Fe Country: A Pictorial Guidebook*. Santa Fe: Sunstone Press, 1978.

———. *Loretto and the Miraculous Staircase*. Santa Fe: Sunstone Press, 1978.

Chávez, Fray Angélico. *But Time and Chance: The Story of Padre Martínez of Taos, 1793–1867*. Santa Fe: Sunstone Press, 1981.

———. *Chávez: A Distinctive American Clan of New Mexico*. Santa Fe: Sunstone Press, 2009. First published 1989.

———. *La Conquistadora: The Autobiography of an Ancient Statue*. Rev. ed. Santa Fe: Sunstone Press, 1983. First published 1954.

———. *My Penitente Land: Reflections on Spanish New Mexico*. Albuquerque: University of New Mexico Press, 1974.

———. *New Mexico Triptych*. Santa Fe: Sunstone Press, 2010. First published 1959.

———. *Our Lady of the Conquest*. Santa Fe: Sunstone Press, 2010. First published 1948.

Chevalier, Jaima. *La Conquistadora, Unveiling the History of a Six Hundred Year Old Religious Icon*. Santa Fe: Sunstone Press, 2010.

Dean, Rob, ed. *Santa Fe, Its 400th Year: Exploring the Past, Defining the Future*. Santa Fe: Sunstone Press, 2010.

De Aragon, Ray John. *The Legend of La Llorona*. Sunstone Press, 2006.

Ebinger, Virginia Nylander. *Aguinaldos: Christmas Customs, Music, and Foods of the Spanish-Speaking Countries of the Americas.* Santa Fe: Sunstone Press, 2008.

Garmhausen, Winona. *History of Indian Arts Education in Santa Fe: The Institute of American Indian Arts, with Historical Background, 1890 to 1962.* Santa Fe: Sunstone Press, 1988.

Hertzog, Peter. *La Fonda: The Inn of Santa Fe.* Santa Fe: Press of the Territorian, 1962.

Hill, R. Kermit Jr. *A New Mexico Primer: For Students of All Ages.* Santa Fe: Sunstone Press, 2011.

Hoefer, Jacqueline. *A More Abundant Life: New Deal Artists and Public Art in New Mexico.* Santa Fe: Sunstone Press, 2003.

Iowa, Jerome. *Ageless Adobe: History and Preservation in Southwestern Architecture.* Santa Fe: Sunstone Press, 1985.

Jaehn, Tomas. Translator, Editor, and Annotator. *The Pastor of New Mexico, Peter Küppers's Memoirs.* Santa Fe: Sunstone Press, 2014

Keleher, William A. *The Fabulous Frontier, 1846–1912.* Santa Fe: Sunstone Press, 2008.

———. *Maxwell Land Grant.* Santa Fe: Sunstone Press, 2008.

———. *Memoirs, Episodes in New Mexico History, 1892–1969.* Santa Fe: Sunstone Press, 2008

———. *Turmoil in New Mexico, 1846–1868.* Santa Fe: Sunstone Press, 2008.

———. *Violence in Lincoln County, 1869–1881.* Santa Fe: Sunstone Press, 2008.

King, Bruce. *Cowboy in the Roundhouse: A Political Life.* Santa Fe: Sunstone Press, 1998.

Lacy, Ann, and Anne Valley-Fox, comps. and eds. *Frontier Stories: A New Mexico Federal Writers' Project Book.* Santa Fe: Sunstone Press, 2010.

———, comps. and eds. *Lost Treasures and Old Mines: A New Mexico Federal Writers' Project Book.* Santa Fe: Sunstone Press, 2011.

———, comps. and eds. *Outlaws and Desperados: A New Mexico Federal Writers' Project Book.* Santa Fe: Sunstone Press, 2008.

———, comps. and eds. *Stories from Hispano New Mexico: A New Mexico Federal Writers' Project Book.* Santa Fe: Sunstone Press, 2012.

———, comps. and eds. *Cowboys, Ranching & Cattle Trails: A New Mexico Federal Writers' Project Book.* Santa Fe: Sunstone Press, 2013

La Farge, Oliver. *Behind the Mountains.* Santa Fe: Sunstone Press, 2008.

———. *Cochise of Arizona.* Santa Fe: Sunstone Press, 2014.

————. *The Enemy Gods*. Santa Fe: Sunstone Press, 2010

————. *The Man with the Calabash Pipe: Some Observations*. Santa Fe: Sunstone Press, 2011.

————. *The Mother Ditch = La Acequia Madre*. Spanish translation by Pedro Ribera Ortega. Santa Fe: Sunstone Press, 1983.

————. *A Pause in the Desert*. Santa Fe: Sunstone Press, 2009

————. *Raw Material: The Autobiographical Examination of an Artist's Journey into Maturity*. Santa Fe: Sunstone Press, 2009.

Lucero, Donald L. *A Nation of Shepherds*. Santa Fe: Sunstone Press, 2004.

————. *In the Dust of Time, An Account of the Pueblo Indian Revolt of 1680 and Its Aftermath*. Santa Fe: Sunstone Press, 2012

————. *The Adobe Kingdom: New Mexico 1598–1958, As Experienced by the Families Lucero de Godoy y Baca*. Santa Fe: Sunstone Press, 2009.

————. *The Rosas Affair*. Santa Fe: Sunstone Press, 2008.

McCulloch, Frank. *Revolution and Rebellion: How Taxes Cost a Governor His Life in 1830s New Mexico*. Illustrations by Frank McCulloch Jr. Santa Fe: Sunstone Press, 2001.

McGeagh, Robert. *Juan de Oñate's Colony in the Wilderness: An Early History of the American Southwest*. Santa Fe: Sunstone Press, 1990.

Martinez, Eluid Levi. *What Is a New Mexico Santo?* Rev. ed. Santa Fe: Sunstone Press, 1992.

Melzer, Richard. *Buried Treasures: Famous and Unusual Gravesites in New Mexico History*. Santa Fe: Sunstone Press, 2007.

————. *Ernie Pyle in the American Southwest*. Santa Fe: Sunstone Press, 1996.

Morand, Sheila. *Santa Fe: Then and Now*. Rev. ed. Santa Fe: Sunstone Press, 2008.

Nusbaum, Jesse L. *Tierra Dulce: Reminiscences from the Jesse Nusbaum Papers*. Santa Fe: Sunstone Press, 1980.

Nusbaum, Rosemary. *The City Different and the Palace: The Palace of the Governors, Its Role in Santa Fe History, Including Jesse Nusbaum's Restoration Journals*. Santa Fe: Sunstone Press, 1978.

Ortega, Pedro Ribera. *Christmas in Old Santa Fe*. 2nd ed. Santa Fe: Sunstone Press, 1973.

————. *La Conquistadora: America's Oldest Madonna*. Santa Fe: Sunstone Press, 1975.

Otero, Miguel Antonio. *My Life on the Frontier, 1864–1882: Incidents and Characters of the Period When Kansas, Colorado, and New Mexico Were Passing through the Last of Their Wild and Romantic Years*. Santa Fe: Sunstone Press, 2007.

———. *My Life on the Frontier, 1882-1897*. Santa Fe: Sunstone Press, 2007.

———. *My Nine Years as Governor of the Territory of New Mexico, 1897–1906*. Facsimile of 1940 edition. Santa Fe: Sunstone Press, 2007.

———. *The Real Billy the Kid*. Santa Fe: Sunstone Press, 2006.

Otero-Warren, Nina. *Old Spain in Our Southwest*. Santa Fe: Sunstone Press, 2006. First published 1936.

Pacheco, Allan. *Ghosts-Murder-Mayhem, A Chronicle of Santa Fe: Lies, Legends, Facts, Tall Tales, and Useless Information*. Santa Fe: Sunstone Press, 2004.

Prince, L. Bradford. *Historical Sketches of New Mexico: From the Earliest Records to the American Occupation*. Facsimile of 1883 edition. Santa Fe: Sunstone Press, 2009.

———. *New Mexico's Struggle for Statehood: Sixty Years of Effort to Obtain Self-Government*. Facsimile of 1910 edition. Santa Fe: Sunstone Press, 2010.

———. *The Student's History of New Mexico*. Santa Fe: Sunstone Press, 2008.

Raciti, James J. *Old Santa Fe: A Brief History, 1536–1912*. Santa Fe: Sunstone Press, 2003.

Sanchez, Richard P., ed. *White Shell Water Place, An Anthology of Native American Reflections on the 400th Anniversary of the Founding of Santa Fe*. Santa Fe: Sunstone Press, 2010.

Scott, Eleanor. *The First Twenty Years of the Santa Fe Opera*. Santa Fe: Sunstone Press, 1976.

Simmons, Marc. *Charles F. Lummis: Author and Adventurer, A Gathering*. Santa Fe: Sunstone Press, 2008.

———. *New Mexico Mavericks: Stories from a Fabled Past*. Santa Fe: Sunstone Press, 2005.

———. *Stalking Billy the Kid*. Santa Fe: Sunstone Press, 2006.

———. *Yesterday in Santa Fe: Episodes in a Turbulent History*. Santa Fe: Sunstone Press, 1989.

Simmons, Marc, and Frank Turley. *Southwestern Colonial Ironwork: The Spanish Blacksmithing Tradition*. Santa Fe: Sunstone Press, 2007.

Siringo, Charles Angelo. *Riata and Spurs: The Story of a Lifetime Spent in the Saddle as Cowboy and Detective*. Santa Fe: Sunstone Press, 2007.

Spinden, Herbert Joseph, tr. *Songs of the Tewa*. Santa Fe: Sunstone Press, 1993.

Stanley, F. *The Civil War in New Mexico*. Santa Fe: Sunstone Press, 2011.

———. *Clay Allison*. Santa Fe: Sunstone Press, 2008.

———. *The Grant That Maxwell Bought*. Santa Fe: Sunstone Press, 2008.

———. *No Tears for Black Jack Ketchum*. Santa Fe: Sunstone Press, 2008.

Stedman, Myrtle, and Wilfred Stedman. *Adobe Architecture*. Santa Fe: Sunstone Press, 1987.

Taylor, Anne. *Southwestern Ornamentation and Design: The Architecture of John Gaw Meem*. Santa Fe: Sunstone Press, 1989.

Twitchell, Ralph Emerson. *The Leading Facts of New Mexico History*. 2 vols. Santa Fe: Sunstone Press, 2007.

———. *The Military Occupation of the Territory of New Mexico from 1846 to 1851*. Santa Fe: Sunstone Press, 2007.

———. *Old Santa Fe: The Story of New Mexico's Ancient Capital*. Santa Fe: Sunstone Press, 2007.

———. *The Spanish Archives of New Mexico*. 2 vols. Santa Fe: Sunstone Press, 2008.

Udall, Sharyn Rohlfsen. *Spud Johnson and Laughing Horse*. Santa Fe: Sunstone Press, 2008.

Wallace, Susan E. *The Land of the Pueblos*. Santa Fe: Sunstone Press, 2006.

Weber, David J. *The Spanish Frontier in North America*. New Haven: Yale University Press, 1992.

West, Elizabeth, ed. *Santa Fe, 400 Years, 400 Questions*. Santa Fe: Sunstone Press, 2012.

Whaley, Charlotte. *Nina Otero-Warren of Santa Fe*. Santa Fe: Sunstone Press, 2007.

When Cultures Meet: Remembering San Gabriel del Yunge Oweenge: Papers from the October 20, 1984 Conference Held at San Juan Pueblo, New Mexico. Santa Fe: Sunstone Press, 1987.

Wurzburger, Rebecca, Tom Aageson, Alex Pattakos, and Sabrina Pratt, eds. *Creative Tourism: A Global Conversation; How to Provide Unique Creative Experiences for Travelers Worldwide*. Santa Fe: Sunstone Press, 2009.

Yoder, Walter D. *The American Pueblo Indian Activity Book*. Santa Fe: Sunstone Press, 1994.

———. *The Big American Southwest Activity Book*. Santa Fe: Sunstone Press, 1997.

———. *The Big Spanish Heritage Activity Book*. Santa Fe: Sunstone Press, 1997.

———. *The Camino Real (The King's Road) Activity Book: Spanish Settlers in the Southwest*. Santa Fe: Sunstone Press, 1994.

———. *The Santa Fe Trail Activity Book: Pioneer Settlers in the Southwest*. Santa Fe: Sunstone Press, 1994.